Elementary Education

Elementary Education

An Easy Alternative to Actual Learning

PATER   MATER   TATER

Mark O'Donnell

Alfred A. Knopf   *New York 1985*

Library of Congress Cataloging in Publication Data

O'Donnell, Mark.
Elementary education.

1. Education—Anecdotes, facetiae, satire, etc.
I. Title.
PS3565.D594E56   1985   818'.5407   85-40229
ISBN 0-394-54430-7

For Stephen—
How do you like it so far?

PORKY: T-t-tell me, Holmes, at what sort of school did you learn to be a detective?

DAFFY (*mangled, defeated, and near death*): Elementary, my dear Watkins, elementary. . . .

Deduce You Say
Warner Bros., 1956

Contents

Letter from the Dean

How did we manage to get all the world's knowledge into one slim volume? Did we in fact manage to get all the world's knowledge into one slim volume?

First, let us consider how all the world's knowledge managed to get into the world. The ancients hallucinated a set of beliefs that they pretended to find satisfactory; their myths were catchy but could not prevent floods. Today we have countered easy ignorance with technology, by its very nature "hard," yet still we yammer in the tempest like yesteryear's troglodytes. Can one book encompass all the callithump and rowdydow of both superstition and data?

Rather than explain, let us stimulate your "Imagination" with this parable, which is mythically if not technically true. There was once a great king who instructed his wise men to bring him all the wisdoms of learning from all corners of the earth so he might possibly use it. His wise men went forth—or at least downstairs—and seven years later presented the king with thousands of books. The king declared he could never read so many books, he wasn't idle like wise men, so the wise men went away again. This time after seven years they brought him a hundred books, but he was fourteen years older than when he first got the idea and was losing steam on it, and he pointed out that he was getting old, a hundred books was too much. The wise men were starting to die off, because they were older than the king to begin with, but the ones remaining went away, to their chambers, I guess, and after seven years they had it down to ten books, just by leaving out all the repetition and frivolousness the hundred books had contained. You're way ahead of me when you picture the old king screaming at the old, old little wise men that he was sick (it had been a bad seven years), and even though it was just ten books, they were still very thick and had lots of very small writing in them, and no index. The wise men had no choice but to retreat to their study and condense all the world's wisdoms into one great heavy tome, so they did, but only one of them was left seven years later to hobble up to the throne room to deliver it. He handed it to the old king and then fell down dead. And right after that the king died, too, without even getting a chance to open the book.

It's been said that if all mankind, and all its knowledge, were liquefied, put in a glass sphere one mile across, balanced on a precipice one mile high, and a bird tried to land on the glass sphere kind of suddenly, no one could guess what would happen because of the hypothetical nature of the experiment. But this book is not hypothetical: birds can land on it. No wise men have condensed it: it's always been this skinny. It may not contain all knowledge, but it's available now, and easy to carry.

Elementary Education

Schoolyard Confidential

You got real big ears, so I hope you know how to listen.

First thing is, don't get scared. If that dog over there smells that you're scared, he'll attack you, so whatever you do don't get scared. Does everybody where you come from have big ears?

Anyway, not getting scared. Just remember the teachers aren't allowed to kill you like in the old days. The principal of this place went on trial once for killing a lot of kids, a whole town of kids, I think. No, some sixth-graders told me. He like made sausages out of them and sold them.

I know what you look like. A beaver. Only with big ears. But don't worry. I'll tell everybody to try not to look at them.

Okay. First of all, if you want any friends you better not say the Pledge of Allegiance exactly right. That's brown-nosing. I always say "invisible with liberty," only sort of in a whisper so they don't catch on I'm doing it. Carl, this kid who was sent home for throwing cleanser at the art teacher, he used to say "Tarnation, underwear, invisible." He even got Maureen Zarzycki to say it, and she always wears white dresses.

That boy over there under the fire escape who smells bad, his mom wears black socks, wait'll you see her. She lets him wear pajama tops instead of shirts. She doesn't know the difference! Maybe they're foreign. You're weird but you're not foreign.

Oh—Did you get my letter? I must have forgotten to *stamp* it! Oops, did I really hurt your foot? See, I had to stamp on your foot when I said stamp. I guess they don't have jokes where you come from.

Here's a Kleenex, don't cry. I only used it to clean my glasses, it's okay. Here, hey, I'll tell you what goes on inside. There's a cloakroom where you put your coat even though nobody ever has a cloak except this kid Carl who came wearing only a blanket on Halloween but he got sent home. Then you sit in this like open cockpit, only there's no dials or knobs on the control panel. I drew some on mine in ink. Pencil's all right for babies, but it isn't forever like ink. I drew them real small so no one will catch on and make me wash them off.

Anyway, you sit at this desk and stuff starts coming at you about vowels and dead guys in wigs and steam. It might be good if it was magic, but it's dumb stuff like why we have winter, and now and then the teacher pretends she has amnesia, and you're supposed to tell her what goes in the blank. You can't really make stuff up, they don't go for that. Like I told Mrs. Griffith how frogs are different from humans because the male lays the eggs and the female fertilizes them.

You don't? Don't you have little sisters or brothers? Wow, it's really awful, wait and I'll tell you about that later.

What we do study is Indians. We've had Indians every year, though who's going to see any, and one year we had them twice because Miss Winnowitz got to go to the hospital for a while and the new teacher didn't know what we'd done already. We churned butter and spread it on Saltines, and Cynthia Noort made a totem pole out of paint cans and trick-or-treat masks, only Carl, this kid who was sent home once for kissing a dog on the mouth during show-and-tell, Carl spilled a whole jar of yellow paint on it and said it was an accident. I like studying Indians.

We're doing the Crusades now. It has to do with spices and people taking boats places by following the arrows. See, I brought these salt and pepper shakers from home as examples of spices. And this is my dad's gun that he keeps in his drawer. I'm doing a play about the Crusades for extra credit.

We did Hitler once, but only as part of something else.

Oh, I hope your mom never throws anything out because we do a lot of stupid art projects, like with jar lids and egg cartons and glitter. One time we were supposed to make butterflies out of paper plates only I had some shoe boxes left from when we were making the Nina, the Pinta, and the Santa Maria, and I made a robot with blood on its teeth and I told Miss Cunningham it was a robot butterfly that had lost its wings but she said I was making her old before her time. There was this one kid named Carl who painted his whole face and said it was for Indians but I think he just wanted to.

There's a curse on the art room anyway, no, there is, because I think there was some kid murdered there a long time ago. We figure it's a curse. Carol Kopp inhaled some ink when she was blowing through a straw to make tree branches on paper from a blob of ink, and she got to go to the dispensary and missed the slides about the food groups, but she saw the posters. Boyd Pavlik got sick eating clay and then he took some home and his brother got sick too. My sister ate some tar out of our driveway but that wasn't for art class. Oh, and this one kid Carl got his hand cut off in the paper cutter only he was just kidding, nothing happened, he used red paint and scrunched his hand up his sleeve, but I still count it as part of the curse.

I'm almost done, you don't have to squirm. Oh. Can you hold it till first bell? Good, I'll go on.

Just hope you never get Miss Deesner. She has everybody draw a picture of themself on a file card and she hangs them across the front of the room and when she's mad at you she turns your picture to the wall. Then at the end of the week whoever's face is left gets a piece of candy, the stuff your mom won't buy because it's too expensive. Not just bull's-eyes. I think both her arms are wood because she wears gloves. She checks fingernails without even warning you the day before. All of a sudden, "Are your nails clean?" It's scary.

What else? You need a quarter every day for chocolate milk. I keep mine in my right front pocket. What are those? Listen, you shouldn't keep marshmallows in your pocket, they lose their shape. Oh, there's first bell.

Oh, and we have this rest period every day after chocolate milk where everybody lies down and turns his head to the right and breathes so no one's breathing in anyone else's face. It's the only thing we have to practice every day.

Einstein Made Even Easier

There's been so much misunderstanding about Einstein's theories of relativity that a scrupulously researched and simply written explanation of his work would be out of place. An uninformed, more intuitive appraisal, however, might just "luck out" in capturing the spirit, if not the technicalities, of relativity, and, granted the luxury of actual misrepresentation and falsification, the body of the great physicist's thought can be rendered simple and even, in some cases, risqué.

First of all, when considering the theories of relativity, concepts like "space," "time," and "matter" are constantly coming up, and unless you're a fast talker, it is essential to understand these terms before trying to impress others.

Time is often depicted as the "fourth dimension," which, though titillating, is giving it a little too much credit. Time is actually nondescript (it has no mass of its own), but it is still surprisingly influential. Perhaps Time can be defined best by an example: A moving body (a debutante, say) is hurled a distance of 40 feet, repeatedly, until sometimes it only makes it 35 feet, and even then on the second or third bounce. If this process takes from 2:00 to 2:45 some afternoon (she may have other appointments to get to), then the motion can be said to have *taken up time,* and you can charge money for it. *Time,* as we observe here, *is what elapses while everything else is going on.*

Space, like Time, is also invisible, but at least it's *there.* If any object moves, or is repossessed, Space takes its place. Try this at home: Move an apple from the table to the refrigerator. Notice the "space" on the table where the apple was? This is Space.

Matter is another matter. It's definitely there, even in the dark, so watch where you step. Matter is sort of the fat old lady that Space and Time play all their pranks on. Einstein's theories involve all three incessantly, and although it's all right to have a favorite, you should be able to deal with all three concepts and keep your preferences to yourself. (Most people prefer Matter, especially on a cold winter's night, though they tend to get Space.)

There are two theories of relativity. The first, or "good" theory, is the one you're thinking of, and has the crowd-pleasing "E = mc^2" sequence. Some observers maintain that Einstein was offered a substantial sum to publish the equation as "E = mc^2 and Pepsi = fine refreshment," but resisted, remarking to a colleague, "It just doesn't swing that way." The second, or "other" theory of relativity, followed up on the success of the first, only that old magic seemed a little wan the second time around. This theory focuses on gravity and acceleration, two subjects that have always been box-office poison.

Einstein began thinking about relativity as a student, when he noticed that the universe "didn't look like itself" in photographs. He realized that this was because nothing is absolutely stationary, and therefore to attempt to measure motion from anywhere was foolish and could induce nausea. Both the observer and the phenomenon observed are always moving around, either toward or away from each other, possibly sinuously, and it's not clear who's leading. Einstein further realized that as objects approach the speed of light, they appear to a relatively still observer to become foreshortened, not to mention blurry. Hence, a clock appears to run slow, a radio seems to drag the rhythm, even on "The Girl from Ipanema," and a jumbo egg seems merely extra-large.

When traveling at the speed of light—and it is best to do so in areas not patrolled by radar—the mass of an object becomes infinite, which makes things crowded for the rest of the objects. This theoretical infinity suggests that *the speed of light is untenable for material objects,* so forget that shutter safari back to the Carboniferous Era. Einstein understood, better perhaps than anyone before and certainly since, that achieving the speed of light requires a lot of initiative, initiative that the average person or jumbo egg doesn't have on its own. Still, the conversion of even the smallest amount of mass (the left eye from a Hummel figure, say) would release an enormous amount of energy, enough to blow up just about any planet that rubbed you the wrong way. Fortunately, bits of matter can't just work themselves up to the speed of light capriciously; the laws of nature require backing and lots of very deliberate scientists with clipboards.

Dr. Guernsey Grater, professor of Endless-Hypothetical-Linoleum-Floors-Stretching-into-Space at the University of Nevada's Center for Meta-Mundane Mathematics, praises Einstein's "humongous intellect," but worries that his theories have not received "the right packaging." Stressing the "liveliness" of energy in his recent book, *The Universe Is It,* Dr. Grater points out that abstract mathematics is "just like a good detective story, only with no plot or characters."

Instead of understanding relativity, therefore, let us attempt to make it interesting. Here is another experiment you can do at home if there is some old energy, mass, and light sitting around. Rocket ships with built-in grandfather clocks are also handy. For this experiment, the two rocket ships must travel away from each other at different speeds, with one eventually reaching the speed of light. Each clock is placed at the rear picture window so the pilot of the other ship can see it, although it may not be a good idea for them to leave the controls to run to the back of the ship to check each other's clocks, especially at the speeds involved. By the way, it would be a lovely dramatic flourish if the pilots could be twins, both for the balanced look of it, and to test the differential aging effect that is one of relativity's more sensational aspects.

Okay. The spaceships separate at dizzying but different speeds. To each pilot, the other ship's clock appears to be running slow. The faster the rockets separate, the slower the other's clock looks, because the image of the clock's face is taking longer to get back to the viewer's eye, and at the speed of light, the clocks look completely halted, all of which brings to mind the sadness of love. In any case, what is amazing about this experiment is not the speed and distance required to conduct it but the incredibly good vision required of the pilots, to see clocks millions of miles away, through the glare of the window and any intervening asteroids. Relativity watching clearly requires a good set of binoculars.

Ultimately, though, one considers modern physics and says, "Well, of course, but besides the *atomic bomb,* where's the percentage? What about using it to stop time so as to stay young and, in my way, beautiful, forever?" It is possible to eliminate aging, at least in others' eyes, by remaining at the speed of light always, though your mass will be infinite (which may affect your looks), and it will be hard for friends to stay in touch. And as regards the spiritually much-italicized atomic bomb: to be fair, relativity existed long before the first man-made nuclear explosion, and it will continue to exist long after the next few, although at that point it will probably have to wend its warped-space way without the flattery of any further mortal commentary.

The Collected Letters of Neanderthal Man

(Undated)

Dear Nina,

I'm sorry not to have written sooner, but I have only recently developed even the most rudimentary powers of reasoning. This makes things easier for me (for example, I know that small rocks are easier to move than large ones) but complicates old burdens as well—not the least of which is the drive to a single-bond formation with another of my species. Ah, Nina, when the flaming bird goes down behind the distant trees and all is blackness, then I wish you were huddled next to me. Often I start up (I can stand on two legs now) thinking I hear your voice, but it is just a wild dog or a boar fallen in a hole. I miss you.

With only the foggiest sense of my own being, I remain,

Gort

(Undated)

Dear Nina,

My painting is making major strides. For instance, I have noticed that animals have four legs (this many: x x x x). This will affect my work enormously. I am no longer doing tracings of my hand, as it seems an inadequate mode of expression. Besides, two of my fingers were bitten off during a heated discussion of art earlier this week.

Stay away from large predators, now!

With primitive passion,

Gort

(Undated)

Dear Nina,

I would be delighted if you could visit me here, but there's another Ice Age due and perhaps we should sit that out.

My *Buffalo Pursued by Hunters* is coming along slowly. The work is draining, and bears enter the cave often while I am working there. I would like to do a bear series someday, showing many wounded, sick, or dead bears in a deep pit. That would please me, and I think it would strike a deeply responsive chord in many others as well. Pardon my shaky hand.

Your own,

Gort

(Undated)

Dear Nina,

Bad, sad news. The last of the dinosaurs died this morning. We'd all thought it had died long ago, which is a poignant comment on its debilitated status. It was a mangy thing, and it lay in some low brush while a taunting circle of opossums threw stones at its eggs. An era has come to an end, Nina: We have no more giants to look up to. Maybe we could pretend there's an even bigger animal that lives in the sky or behind it—something like that. That would be fun. Should we give It teeth, or pretend It's more like a giant clam? But I realize people will ask to see Its droppings before they believe in It. Since we developed opposable thumbs, everybody feels like he has to clutch a thing for it to be real.

Well, dear one, stay as high on the evolutionary ladder as you are, and don't eat any green berries!

Hugs and a severe clubbing,

Gort

(Undated,
though adhering food
fragments help date the
letter at 35,000 B.C.)

Dear Nina,

This afternoon I stopped off for a cooling drink at the new Pond in the Barren Waste (you remember, we used to go there with Nick when it was the Pond in the Forest, before the fire), when who should kneel on the bank beside me but Cro-Magnon Man. I'd heard a lot about him and seen his work (he did the pots I was telling you about), but I never imagined we'd have this "historic" meeting. He's much less hairy than you'd suppose from the vitality of his work, and he has a conceptual glint in his eye that's quite striking.

I introduced myself with a diplomatic chest-pound, which I'm afraid he took amiss. He asked why I wasn't extinct yet and criticized my low brow ridge. I was hurt, but as a fellow savage I can understand how one gets into these moods. I grabbed a fish from the water and took a bite from it before offering it to him as a peace gesture. Evidently he is one of those fire faddists, because he refused it. So I send what remains along to you.

It's a pity our first encounter was so mixed, because I had hoped the two of us could share an exhibition of our work. I never could do pots.

My regards to your offspring.

Yours in primitive superstition,
Gort

(Undated)

Dear Nina,

Fate has dealt me a cruel blow. Just before my one-man show was to open here, a plague gripped our community, carrying off all but me. I attribute my survival to my recent invention of the complete breakfast.

I opened the show anyway, but no one has entered except some bears. Again, I apologize for the uneven hand, but a recent accident (I was trying to cook a fish) has put my right hand out of commission.

I know there's snow on the ground now, but I'd love it if you came to visit. Bring food.

Love,
Gort

(Undated)

Dear Nina,

I may not be writing to you much longer. I can hear some unknown tribe pounding on drums and blowing horns in the distance. Everything seems so strange. I just can't seem to adapt.

All day today I wanted to draw a mastodon, but I hunted all over the hillside and even across where the river used to be and couldn't find one. The kids over there have never even heard of mastodons, or at least that's what they pretended.

Again, pardon the wobbly hand, but I have a lot of bruises from hurled stones. There go the drums again. I wish I'd learned an instrument.

My love to little Flint. Tell her what a big strong man is coming to see her soon!

Eternally yours,
Gort

P.S. Why have you not been answering my letters?

Neanderthal Man went extinct in 34,998 B.C., three weeks after this letter was sent. He is survived by Modern Man. Nothing he wrote was published in his lifetime.

The inventor of fire and of the complete breakfast was placed in an unknown tomb or possibly eaten.

His dogs were observed to miss him.

Correct English in the Home

Gretchen.—Mother, mayn't I go outside? I ain't been bad.

Mrs. R.—You mean you *haven't* been bad, Gretchen, but if that's how you choose to speak, then you have been.

Gretchen.—But I'm awful, I mean, *awfully* sick of this one room.

Junius.—It's rude to criticize, isn't it, Mother?

Mrs. R.—That's right, Junius, especially one's mother. And one says *very*, not *awfully*, unless you really are awful.

Junius.—We're lucky to have a mother who puts her own real-life children and their real-life conversation in her lovely grammar books.

Mrs. R.—I've always felt people preferred *true* stories. When I was a girl, and my stepmother told me something, I always asked, "Is it *true?*" I was afraid she would lie to me.

Junius.—In most lessons you have us ask you about your girlhood, Mother.

Mrs. R.—I'll do that now.

Gretchen.—Mama, tell us again about the party where you got more candy than any other girl!

Mrs. R.—Say *Mother*, Gretchen, not *Mama*. You are no baby, although you wet your bed often enough!

Gretchen.—Did you haff to include that in the lesson, for everyone to read!

Mrs. R.—Did I *have* to, Gretchen? No. But I've always felt

people preferred *true* stories, even when learning correct English for the home.

Junius.—Like that story of you and the pretty girls.

Mrs. R.—Yes, stories *such as* that one.

Gretchen.—You sat alone in a corner, because you were so *very* large-boned.

Junius.—And you cried and cried and cried because everyone was so unfair to you, who were so smart and knew how to converse.

Mrs. R.—Junius uses *were* very well, doesn't he, Gretchen?

Gretchen.—Yes, for someone only five years old.

Mrs. R.—Here, Junius, I have untied your feet. But don't stamp them on the floor as you sit. Be polite.

Gretchen.—I wish *I* was untied.

Mrs. R.—Do you wish you *were* untied, Gretchen?

Gretchen.—(*does not speak*)

Junius.—Anyway, the grown-up lady running the party gave you candy to make you stop, and you got more candy than any of the girls who didn't cry.

Gretchen.—And more toys.

Mrs. R.—No, Gretchen, that is a lie. There were no toys.

Gretchen.—You always have me say the wrong thing.

Mrs. R.—Gretchen, you are so like your father, who disappeared.

Gretchen.—I wish *I* were to disappear!

Mrs. R.—Good, Gretchen, *were* is correct. *Will* I untie one of your feet? Or *shall* I?

Gretchen.—You untied *both* of Junius's feet!

Mrs. R.—I can trust Junius not to run away.

Gretchen.—I won't neither.

Junius.—Mama says we are to say *either* with *not* verbs or their contractions.

Mrs. R.—*Mother*, Junius. And it should be pronounced *eye-ther*, as the wealthy British do, to rhyme with "scyther," one who scythes, you've seen paintings of Death in his hood.

Gretchen.—I wish I didn't have to wear a blindfold *eye-ther*.

Mrs. R.—No, you are too like your father, who disappeared, Gretchen. The sight of flesh would excite you too much. You would run away.

Gretchen.—I wish I could see even once the rabbits Junius said have been on the lawn all week.

Junius.—Everyone of them is gone now.

Gretchen.—*Are* gone—Right, Mother?

Mrs. R.—No, Gretchen. *They are* gone, but *everyone is* gone.

Gretchen.—You mean, they *are* gone?

Mrs. R.—All *are*, everyone *is*.

Gretchen.—You mean they *aren't*?

Mrs. R.—It's the dead of night. The rabbits are in their holes.

Gretchen.—Tell us again about the time you showed up that conceited lady from the hospital.

Mrs. R.—All right.

Gretchen.—I hate it when you have me ask questions like— *such as*—that.

Mrs. R.—Polite people never say *hate*, Gretchen.

Gretchen.—But when you talk about Daddy—

Mrs. R.—I do not talk about your father.

Gretchen.—But you *do!*

Mrs. R.—Since you insist on being bad—

Gretchen.—No, Mother! Tell us about the conceited lady, it was Miss—

Mrs. R.—Never mind; you should not mention names in criticizing persons.

Junius.—She came here *as if* to take you someplace where they don't write lovely true grammar books with their real children in them.

Mrs. R.—That is true. People prefer true stories.

Junius.—And you showed her! You pretended not to see her!

Gretchen.—You acted like she was invisible!

Mrs. R.—No, I acted *as if* she *were* invisible.

Gretchen.—You write me as more stupid than I am.

Mrs. R.—Yes, *as*. It's to encourage my readers.

Junius.—Since you are writing this, Mother, I ask you to finish the story I've heard so many times before, about the conceited lady you pretended not to see or hear.

Mrs. R.—You may as well tell it yourselves, children.

Junius.—You cried and cried, but she *didn't* give you *any* candy.

Mrs. R.—That's right, she *gave* me *none*.

Gretchen.—Then you axed her to stay.

Mrs. R.—Correct, for once, Gretchen.

The Laws of Cartoon Motion

1. Any body suspended in space will remain suspended in space until made aware of its situation.

Daffy Duck steps off a cliff, expecting further pastureland. He loiters in midair, soliloquizing flippantly, until he chances to look down. At this point, the familiar principle of 32 feet per second per second takes over.

2. Any body in motion will tend to remain in motion until solid matter intervenes suddenly.

Whether shot from a cannon or in hot pursuit on foot, cartoon characters are so absolute in their momentum that only a telephone pole or an outsize boulder retards their forward motion absolutely. Sir Isaac Newton called this sudden termination the stooge's surcease.

3. Any body passing through solid matter will leave a perforation conforming to its perimeter.

Also called the silhouette of passage, this phenomenon is the specialty of victims of direct-pressure explosions and reckless cowards who are so eager to escape that they exit directly through the wall of a house, leaving a cookie-cutout-perfect hole. The threat of skunks or matrimony often catalyzes this reaction.

4. The time required for an object to fall twenty stories is greater than or equal to the time it takes for whoever knocked it off the

*ledge to spiral down twenty flights to attempt to capture it un-
broken.*

Such an object is inevitably priceless, the attempt to capture
it inevitably unsuccessful.

5. *All principles of gravity are negated by fear.*

Psychic forces are sufficient in most bodies for a shock to pro-
pel them directly away from the surface. A spooky noise or an
adversary's signature sound will induce motion upward, usually to
the cradle of a chandelier, a treetop, or the crest of a flagpole. The
feet of a running character or the wheels of a speeding auto need
never touch the ground, ergo fleeing turns to flight.

6. *As speed increases, objects can be in several places at once.*

This is particularly true in tooth-and-claw fights, in which a
character's head may be glimpsed emerging from a cloud of alter-
cation at several places simultaneously. This effect is common as
well among bodies that are spinning or being throttled, and simulates our own vision's trailing retention of images. A "wacky"
character has the option of self-replication only at manic high
speeds and may ricochet off walls to achieve the velocity required
for self-mass-liberation.

7. *Certain bodies can pass through a solid wall painted to resemble tunnel entrances; others cannot.*

This trompe-l'oeil inconsistency has baffled generations, but
at least it is known that whoever paints an entrance on a wall's
surface to trick an opponent will be unable to pursue him into this
theoretical space. The painter is flattened against the wall when
he attempts to follow into the painting. This is ultimately a problem of art, not of science.

8. *Any violent rearrangement of feline matter is impermanent.*

Cartoon cats possess more deaths than even the traditional
nine lives afford. They can be sliced, splayed, accordion-pleated,

spindled, or disassembled, but they cannot be destroyed. After a few moments of blinking self-pity, they reinflate, elongate, snap back, or solidify.

9. *For every vengeance there is an equal and opposite revengeance.*

This is the one law of animated cartoon motion that also applies to the physical world at large. For that reason, we need the relief of watching it happen to a duck instead.

The Search for Unhappiness

I've heard it said that into every life some rain must fall. I really have. None of the great stories are pure happiness all the way through, especially the *really* great ones, if you get the picture. Unfortunately, the story of my friend Tony is not only unrelenting in how happy it is, it gets even happier as it goes along.

THE STORY ITSELF

Tony had everything you could want without outside coaching. His parents were tranquil, he was always popular, and his good manners caused school board officials to make fools of themselves over him. When he graduated second in our class (luckily for him, because we always threw mud at the valedictorian out of resentment), everyone predicted his future would be bright. How wrong they were to underestimate him.

Of course, he didn't want unsullied happiness. It seemed inconsiderate. So, he tried various get-wretched-quick schemes, but they kept working out fine in the end. First he fell in with the wrong crowd, people who laughed at responsibility and dressed to hurt their mothers, but he was quickly sought out for product endorsements and upscale dinner parties. The wrong crowd was very revered in our town. I hoped against hope that their thoughtless caprices would at least hurt his feelings, but Tony always ended up laughing at their childishness.

Then he tried to run through his vast inheritance, but once he demonstrated he had money, he was invited everywhere for free and was sent goodwill gifts from local merchants. He gambled and drank, but you can imagine how the former turned out, and our street corner singing fueled by the latter landed him a major vocal recording contract. That was the same night I was arrested for disturbing the peace.

I suggested he try the military (an idea that proves I could hold my own in one of those think tanks where they earn more in one shrug than I make in a year at the mill), and Tony would have taken my typically free suggestion, except that his radical grandparents, who had made millions in marriage manuals, made him too undependable in the local recruiters' eyes. It was a blow to his potential unhappiness.

Then I suggested he give all his worldly goods and coupons to me and let the community take his tailspin from there. Unfortunately, he would have been only too happy to do that for me, his old friend, so he decided it would be better not to, since the whole problem was that he was Only Too Happy already. Was his reasoning sophistical? It's not for me to judge if he was incredibly wrong, more wrong than anyone ever since time began, so I won't.

Some people squirm at this point and suggest that Tony could have done harm to himself. The way they look at me I sometimes think they wish I'd take the same hint. The answer is *Yes,* he could have done harm to himself. But he wasn't *unwell,* like people who suggest that. He didn't want pain, stop making me repeat this. He wanted the scope, the whole alphabet, the woof and the tweet, the peep and the roar, the rest of the menu.

Then Tony proposed to the most awful woman (you can look her up in the Guinness book), and for a while it seemed not to go just beautifully. But she insisted on going to Burma to have a bridal jacket of human bones made. A year went by with no word from her, though gossips whispered he was happier than ever before. Finally he received a brick in the mail, postage due, from

Kuala Lumpur. We figured she had drifted to a new love and was
saying goodbye—there was a bite taken out of it.

The whole exploring-live-volcanoes period that followed bears
no discussion, except with my insurance people, who still fight
my claim by pointing out that my companion was completely un-
harmed. And as for gratuitous vacant insults to burly strangers, I
guess his was a kind of charm that could carry it off. I can't, myself.

No, there was only one thing left for Tony to do.

SURPRISE ENDING

What it was I'm not going to tell you.

QUESTIONS FOR DISCUSSION

(1) Is it ours to decide if there is any true, surefire path to
Unhappiness? Discuss the possibilities among yourselves.

(2) Is True Unhappiness something we will only know in the
afterlife?

EXTRA CREDIT

Recite Tony's name hundreds of times, stealthily, continuously, to
yourself. Tighten your belt until you see little stars and planets
swimming before your eyes. Finally, see all life as mindlessly rep-
licating molecules. Or, build a little Eskimo village out of egg-
shells.

Dilly in De Basement

(*A tiny porno shop, with racks and shelves of brightly colored magazines and marital aids. Dilly, a spirited little girl in a jumper and frilly blouse, enters and addresses the kindly old shopkeeper, Mr. Fleischmann. A shop-bell tinkles as she enters.*)

DILLY: Good morning, Mr. Fleischmann!

MR. FLEISCHMANN: Mornin', Dilly.

DILLY: Sold any porno today?

MR. FLEISCHMANN (*indicating the empty store*): Nope. Folks ain't buyin' like they useta.

DILLY: Aww, why not?

MR. FLEISCHMANN: Some dream inside 'em has died, I guess.

DILLY (*wandering into the store's aisle*): . . . Momma says it's a world gone mad, but only when I hit her. Gosh, what a lot of funny things!

MR. FLEISCHMANN: You just take care there, Dilly! Crazy child . . . (*She is out of his line of sight now, behind a rack of books*)

DILLY: What's this? . . . (*phone rings*)

MR. FLEISCHMANN (*answering phone*): Pop's Porno Corner . . . No, we have the human ones, though. . . . (*Suddenly, Dilly tumbles through a sliding trap door, unseen by the shopkeeper*)

DILLY: Help! (*She is gone. All is as before*)

MR. FLEISCHMANN (*into phone*): Yes, we mail it in a plain brown box. Sure thing, your honor. (*Hangs up*) Dilly? She

25

musta run outside. That crazy girl! (*Pause*) Hmm—Saturday. Where are all the schoolteachers? (*Weird harp chord, fadeout. Lurid red light comes up on De Basement, a dark, unwholesome anti-candyland, outlandish yet flimsy, and cluttered like a Hieronymus Bosch nightmare. A giant, jagged-ended candy cane suggests the demoralized "fantasy" of this skew, ruined world, as though ravaging children had decimated it. A monstrous strand of DNA, like a funhouse staircase, winds aimlessly behind. Dilly enters as if from a fall down a long chute. She looks around and sees a sort of animal-eared troll tending a bubbling brew, who ogles her lasciviously; he holds a puffy, vaguely pitchforked staff. An infuriating disco beat plays throughout, though at blessedly low volume*)

DILLY (*smelling dank fumes*): Whoa! Whew! Ugh! . . . Where am I? What *is* this place? (*The troll, a Peter Lorre pop-eyed crazy, grins*)

TROLL (*relishing this*): . . . De basement!

DILLY: You mean *the, the* basement, yes? (*Troll slavers repellently*) No?

TROLL (*slowly*): Deese . . . ees . . . dee . . . basement!

DILLY: Whew, that's for sure! Is there a way out?

TROLL (*mysteriously*): Only one.

DILLY: Well?

TROLL: You don't want to *die*, surely?

DILLY (*annoyed*): This is useless. (*She looks around on her own*) Are you some kind of lost Hottentot, or pygmy, or what? (*She wanders into a pile of trash*) Ugh! Empty shoe boxes! (*She sees the bent giant shard of candy cane*) That candy is *spoiled!* (*Turns*) Oh! Who are you! (*Three forlorn yet feverish shapes wiggle at her like doughy fingers in a glove. They are the demonic counterpart of Wonderland stage "flowers" with people inside. They are barely mobile, and though raptly tuned to Dilly, they never look at each*

*other or acknowledge each other, even though they speak
together)*

ALL THREE (*in entranced unison*): We are the lonesome gametes!

DILLY: Gametes?

ALL THREE: Sperm. Eggs. The lonesome gametes.

DILLY (*scientifically*): You speak in unison. Do you sing, too?

ALL THREE (*They sing, in harmony, to the wretched disco beat*):
We are the lonesome gametes,
only half a normal cell.
How we long to be a zygote,
DNA, O then all will be well!
(Bein' half is hell!)

(*Pose, as if for applause*)

DILLY: You know, it's not as simple as all that.

FIRST GAMETE: That was from our Christmas Spectacular.

DILLY: I missed it.

TROLL (*hobbling up eagerly*): She ees new to De Basement!
(*grins*) She's only twelve!

SECOND GAMETE (*after a pause*): We may be coarse, but *he's*
disgusting!

DILLY: Is this an alternate universe, is that the idea?

TROLL: She wants to *leave! Leave* De Basement! (*Laughs*)

THIRD GAMETE: Oh you can't leave, Miss. You're our slave.

DILLY (*She knows her rights*): That's ridiculous!

THIRD GAMETE (*agreeably*): It is. And degrading.

SECOND GAMETE: In a lot of ways. (*belches*)

FIRST GAMETE (*fervently, to her*): I'm so lonesome! (*tries to
nuzzle her*)

DILLY (*She's had enough*): I'm leaving! It looks shabby enough
to bust out of! Unless it's, like, magic! (*She looks around,
readying herself to escape*)

ALL THREE GAMETES: Don't! We'll give you a dollar to stay!

DILLY (*not impressed*): A dollar. Let's see the dollar.

ALL THREE GAMETES: Well . . . (*They look sheepishly back and forth to each other. They haven't got it. Then, they turn to her*) Go on then, if you think you can.

DILLY: My pleasure!

ALL THREE GAMETES (*wriggling excitedly*): Pleasure!

DILLY: Stupid gametes! (*But she can find no way to mount the warped DNA staircase*)

TROLL (*approaching with a cup of the noxious brew*): You weel never escape! Never! Eeet ees your *life!!!!* (*to gametes*) Hold her! Compel her! Obsess her!

DILLY (*pluckily, as they swarm about her*): You're nothing but a pack of chemicals! (*She gives a little scream, half of fright and half of anger. Blackout. Pause. We come back to the sunlit porno parlor. Dilly tumbles back in, among the dildos and harnesses*)

DILLY (*surprised*): Whoa!! I—I—Mr. Fleischmann!

MR. FLEISCHMANN: Dilly! Where'd you pop up from?

DILLY (*Runs to him and hugs him*): Oh Mr. Fleischmann, is it ever good to be back home!

MR. FLEISCHMANN: Dilly, were you *asleep* back there?

DILLY: Aw, I—you'd never believe me!

MR. FLEISCHMANN (*warmly tousling her hair*): Oh, I don't know. After fifty years in the porno business, I can believe anythin'!

DILLY (*patronizingly, as an adult to a child; it's her secret*): Oh, it's a big world, Mr. Fleischmann, you might be surprised! (*Pose. Funny sentimental chord. Blackout.*)

Semiverbal Communication

An Oriental man is sitting alone in a restaurant, sadly eating apple pie and coffee. Clearly, he only knows how to order "apple pie and coffee." It is the only English phrase he has learned. What if some understanding waitress with nails as red as roses brought him veal cutlets when he ordered "apple pie and coffee"? He would be grateful, and return every day, as she brought him omelettes, salads, steaming newborn roasts—all from orders for "apple pie and coffee." They would smile at each other, since they could not converse. She would give him credit for what he was willing to mean. They would go dancing and ask the band to play "Apple Pie and Coffee." The parade of days would pass. All seas would retreat. They would marry and have rose-red Oriental children. When evening came, the children would play on the darkling lawn, shouting "Apple pie and coffee." The stars would divulge themselves above the trees. Life would be worthwhile.

Insect Societies

Listen, don't talk to me about bees. Soldier bees, worker bees, none of 'em. I'm on to those bees. They have their own language, for starters. Sure. You think I'm kidding? Bees can talk. They did a study on it. You didn't know that? Scientists can talk to the bees the same way they talk to Flipper. They just put on their head-phones and turn on their computer-translators and start chatting up the bees like nobody's business. True. They've been talking to the bees for years. They just don't let that fact get out because there'd be panics.

In fact, it was the bees who invented the A-bomb. Sure. You think a man could've invented the A-bomb? Naah. It takes a bug to come up with something like that.

Oh, they're smart, I give them that much. Very keen, those little feelers are always working. I heard how the scientists study the bee brain and model the computers after it. But you won't read that fact in the evening paper. They couldn't let a fact like that get out. They couldn't. There would be panics.

One thing those bees have come up with is a time-travel bomb. It is the perfect ultimate weapon. In case somebody ever bombs us first, we send the time-travel bomb back in time and it bombs them before they can bomb us, so we never get bombed. Pretty good, huh? We may have to wait a little to find out if it really works.

Anyway, bees are all geniuses. They even have little built-in glasses they wear. But it's just like the UFOs, they do a cover-up job on it. Just like you could get gas for a penny a gallon if they used this pill that was invented. You didn't know that? You didn't know that? Sure. You drop it in water. But the big oil companies do a big cover-up on it. Just like the birth control fog they have that could cover a whole city (or just a neighborhood, if you get my meaning). Then you'd have to go through a lot of paper work before you could have a baby. You'd have to be really serious about it. But the baby-bootie concerns do a big cover-up on it.

You didn't know that? It's just the tip of the corruption iceberg. Everybody's on the take, schoolteachers (from the Russians), the cops (I think the government pays them).

I know what you think. You think you can ask the President for help. Forget that. Don't ask him for help, he doesn't know who you are. Who are you, a schmo, nothing personal. Don't ask him for help. He doesn't even answer his own mail, he has people to do it. People answer his mail, not him. You could be dead and ask him for help and he wouldn't hear you.

Presidents try to kill themselves all the time, you know. There's so much pressure, it's like they're prisoners. True. Every President since the Hoover Administration has been constantly trying to kill himself. But they hush it up. Who needs panics? They have to strap his arms to his side so he won't start doing harm to himself. Don't offer me that job, boy, you can have it! I don't even want it! But they don't show the straps when he's on TV.

Half the time those Presidents are in the hospital, begging to be allowed to die. But they have to go on, they're forced to. You and I—Who are we? John Q. Schmo—we never hear about it. That's not the President you see on TV anyway. He's in the critical ward somewhere. That's his double you see on TV.

Sure. You didn't know that? That's his double. You don't think they would let the President of the United States go out and stand in the open where he could be shot! They have too much money invested in him to do that.

Of course, all those guys have doubles, too, to make their

speeches. You didn't know that? You didn't know that? Everybody big gets a double. It's all done with plastic surgery.

Those aren't the movie stars themselves you see up there on the movie screen, either. Naah. That's their doubles. And everything they say is written out for them. They have people to do their conversation. And the weather lady on the phone? That's not her. They use somebody else's voice. Some schmo's. But the movie stars sleep late and who pays the millions of dollars in income taxes for the plastic surgery for their doubles? You and me, the little guy, the schmo on the graveyard shift who has to eat his lunch at three in the morning, the worker, the drone. So don't talk to me about bees.

THE OLD
CODGER'S
1985
ALMANAC

— Weather forecasts —
for all lost or stalled motorists whether they
want them or not

LETTER TO PATRONS

Here at the watershed roadside offices of *The Old Codger's Almanac*, we have several complete sets of all 486 previous editions of the little volume you are now holding, and all of us here must say we enjoy browsing through the stacks of these old troves of information. Crops Editor Bert Winters and I, for one, often abandon our families and checkers partners for weeks on end to bone up on some particularly arresting stretches of decades. (Did you know, for instance that in 1805, the tide went out but not in?)

The annual news of the sun's and moon's movements may lack the sensation and splash of more trivial journalism, but there is a soothing, musical regularity to the long rows of statistics that I myself prefer to warm Ovaltine. So we continue, year after year, like the running of the sap, undaunted by time, weather, and the fickleness of changing design styles. "Why do you maintain this illegible, crackerbarrel rigamarole in this day and age?" I am asked by lost media people from New York who mistake our offices for a gas station. "The layout is dense, it's unfocused and frankly unattractive," they tend to go on. "Maybe," I respond, "but I ain't the one who's lost."

This is not to say we haven't been tempted over the years to offer more timely material than kitchen remedies and unsolicited advice. Our 1943 and 1944 editions, in addition to a Pony Express retrospective, featured detailed articles on the interior designs and present positions of all battleships in the American fleet.

Since then, we have made occasional forays into the appraisal of passing fads (e.g., *Ten Uses for Old Television Antennas*, 1962), but, for the most part, we sit tight under the rapture of stars like a contented, abandoned plow.

Still, we have our own measure of fashionability. These days, what with every taxi-taking ballet dancer and advertising executive gallivanting around in down-filled skivvies and a hunter's jacket, eating country-style anything, discussing their window-boxes, and talking down-home talk into C.B.'s, *The Old Codger's Almanac* has had something of a slow-blooded revival. A lot of folks hang it in their summer home like a social register.

So, if anything, the incomprehensibility of the book boosts its value as a status accessory. And a lot of people find comfort in the notion that the elements themselves can be camp.

However that may be, we press on, already gathering outdated information for next year's edition. By our fruits ye shall know us, and by yours.

FEBRUARY hath 30 days.

1985

> The winter wind will drone and drone
> From day's debut 'til night is black:
> Its sound is very like the tone
> Of The Old Codger's Almanac.

D.M.	D.W.	Dates, Feasts, Fasts, Aspects, Taxes Due	Weather	Farmer's Calendar
1	M.	**CIRCUMCISION** ● Taxes {$10.50 / $11.70	*Snow,*	Remove drifts of snow that have accumulated indoors and investigate possible missing walls.
2	Tu.	☾ over Miami ● *stupid birds come north*	*sleet*	
3	W.	**All Saints Softball** ● ●!☛ Taxes {$9.25 / $10.10	*and slop*	Dip all household articles in tar to preserve them.
4	Th.	☾ *light becomes you* ● 1st woman lawyer dies, 1892	*on top*	Old Christmas trees can be used to cover floors with festive dry needles.
5	Fr.	Rhode Island ignored, 1925 ● Taxes {$10.75 / $10.75	*of ice:*	
6	Sa.	How high the ☾ ● *Jupiter lets Mars lead*	*not neat*	Slice enough cheese for the entire winter, in case frostbitten fingers prevent knife use later.
7	**G**	**St. Elmo's Fire Sale** ● Taxes {$9.50 / $11.00	*or nice —*	
8	M.	Festival of the Related-by-Marriage Gleaners	*Watch out!*	
9	Tu.	largest whale born, 1881 ● *Pluto does a little dance*	*Winds clout*	Get up at half-hour intervals throughout the night to shake the bottled salad dressings in the refrigerator. This will prevent even momentary settling of contents.
10	W.	old devil ☾ ● *frogs stir in sleep*	*your home*	
11	Th.	1st tub in White House, 1938 ● Taxes {$11.05 / $12.05	*and chill*	
12	Fr.	Elizabeth Taylor born, 1932	*goodwill*	
13	Sa.	Elizabeth Taylor born again (for photographers), 1932	*'til all*	
14	**G**	52nd Sunday after last year ● ☾ *river*	*within,*	Leftover holiday guests make perfect sources of inconvenience and unpleasantness.
15	M.	*Saturn arrested for trespassing by Venus*	*their*	
16	Tu.	it's only a paper ☾ ● snow in Alaska, 1926	*patience*	Moose and bear can be coaxed into the house to spend winter with you by coating the halls and staircases with maple syrup.
17	W.	**All Goats Day** ● meteor resembling Will Rogers, 1953	*thin,*	
18	Th.	☾ *light sonata* ● 4-foot herring elected to Congress, 1938	*lash at*	
19	Fr.	fly me to the ☾ ● Unknown Soldier's birthday	*each other,*	
20	Sa.	*moon eclipsed by large building*	*husband. mother*	
21	**G**	D. Eisenhower either b. or d., not clear which	*children, wife.*	Catch all local mice and rabbits and pull their teeth to prevent garden damage come spring.
22	M.	Lint Day !$%&* ● Taxes {$11.30 / $12.00	*and life*	
23	Tu.	unexplained noises, 1840 ● $◐♂	*seems ghastly.*	
24	W.	**Doomed Wheat Day** ● Taxes {$9.75 / $10.60	*Lastly,*	Label your children and store them in a dry, frostproof place.
25	Th.	☾ glow ● St. Anne's Surprise Potluck	*though,*	
26	Fr.	Bad News Day ● *frogs murmur spouses' name*	*a thaw!*	Use the mild, moonlit nights to prune grapevines and dig up a disliked neighbor's garden.
27	Sa.	concept for Star Wars born, 1974 ♣♡●	*Hurrah!*	
28	**G**	**Gherkin Sunday** ● *Aquarius aligns with rich relatives*	*Then*	Chip away at large boulders with only a needle, to learn better what eternity means.
29	M.	Deodorizing of St. Jerome ● Taxes {$10.45 / $11.00	*more*	
30	Tu.	☾ comes over the mountain ● world ends, 1979	*snow.*	

S T A T E · F A I R

Thank you for the peaches Cling,
Thank you for the cherries Bing,
Thank you for the Kong that's King
Thank you, God, for everything.
— TRADITIONAL GRACE

PRIZE-WINNING JAMS AND JELLIES ARE AS NEAR AS YOUR NEAREST GOURMET STORE

by Velveteena Tinbrook Wheeler

Yes, mealtime wouldn't be meal time without food, and few foods are as nice as good jams and jellies, just as the little prayer above suggests. Delicious on bread, all by itself in bowls (I serve it in troughs on New Year's Eve instead of alcohol), or packed inside a big Christmas Turkey and/or doughnut, jams and jellies have long been truly the "staff of life" for millions. Even the ancient Egyptians must have loved their jelly, because we certainly don't find any leftovers cluttering up their tombs!

The best method I know for making preserves is quick, inexpensive and sure to snare you a blue ribbon at your next State Fair. I would, of course, be a fool to part with it, so I'll tell you a lesser recipe which should, nonetheless, suit your purposes adequately.

First of all, remember that when making fruit preserves, fruit is of the essence. In these strapped times, it's a temptation just to churn out the preserves minus the expense of fruit, but even if your guests don't catch on, you'll know in your heart you've been cheap — and anyway, if you like bright colors in your kitchen creations, you'll want that extra sparkle that ingredients always add.

Now that you've peeled and sliced a load of peaches or raspberries — I usually gauge a winter's supply by how many it takes to snap the springs on my mother-in-law's daybed — put on some water to boil. This is for coffee, since you've been doing all that thankless peeling and slicing for hours without a break.

Refreshed? Back to work, this time to cook those peeled and sliced whatevers within an inch of their soulless lives. Then, add sugar, pectin, cornstarch and perhaps some storebought jelly as an encouraging example to the rest of the mixture. After that — by the way, I hope you used *clean* jars! We don't want bolts or bandaids in among the boysen berries — it'll be no time before blue ribbons are dangling on your prize preserves.

Remember, too, that sometimes your own excellence is not so effective as preventing the excellence of others. Switching labels at the judging booth can make strawberry jam look deathly green, and green beans seem a bloody pulp. A little well-timed jostling and your neighbors won't even be in the running, except for a mop and wastebasket. In that gingham dress you're wearing and your hair pulled back in a bun, no one will imagine that the corridors of evil in your heart are as labyrinthine as a city slicker's.

And, after all, isn't that the beauty of country life?

RAINY DAY AMUSEMENTS

—PAPER SCRUNCHING—

Those with no patience for origami can use scrunched-up paper and lots of glue to fashion assorted animal or human figures, mostly very basic snowmen. Paper scrunching is an art that has been unknown to the Orient for centuries and though they tend to resemble stuck-together popcorn balls, scrunched-up paper figures often give the maker minutes of satisfaction.

——WUT WUZZAT?——

Alone? Blindfold yourself and spin until you are dizzy. Now, walk around the house colliding with things. Carry a pad of paper and scribble down what you imagine you've broken, based on the sound of the objects crashing to the floor. When exhausted, stop, have something cool to drink, and compare the real breakage with your guesses. The ears, you'll find, are not as quick as the eye.

——BRAIN TAUNTERS——

Mr. Morton wants to combine candy costing 79 cents a pound with candy costing 99 cents a pound to get a mixture costing 87 cents a pound. Is that all right with you?

John and Jane live on a planet that is 8,000 miles in diameter hurtling through space at 1,800 miles a second, tipped 23½° to the plane of its orbit. What chance does their love have?

THE TEN MOST COMMON ARGUMENTS—SETTLED

- The chicken came first, not the egg.
- Hot tea does not cool you off.
- Not even the President can hold his breath for more than three minutes.
- You cannot get used to poison.
- Fish *do* feel pain when hooked, but who cares?
- Scarlett does not get Rhett back.
- There are no top-secret federal conferences with super-intelligent bees.
- Women are more neat than men, except unmarried ones in large cities.
- You cannot get drunk on water, no matter how much you drink.
- It is not proper to machine-wash the American flag. It *is* proper not to mention that it is dirty.

ANSWERS TO LAST YEAR'S PUZZLES

(1) First of all, hens can't talk. Second, even if they could, they wouldn't go around trading their own eggs. No answer is correct.

(2) No, because we didn't tell you that the mother didn't really die. She was all right all along.

(3) Seven in all. There will be no Leap Year in 2200, don't forget.

(4) It depends.

(5) Never. Don't forget, the water would flow down the drain the other way once the bathtub crossed the equator.

(6) Five pieces, if you think you could eat that many.

(7) None—since, you'll recall, penguins live only at the *South* Pole.

(8) Ten. Or eleven, if you jammed them in.

(9) An infinite amount, but it sounds like publicity to us.

(10) Farmer Jones should reply, "I don't give a tinker's cuss about your daughter being half the age you are now and my being twice your age next year. I asked you a civil question and I expect a direct answer, dammit."

Groundhog's Day

The zoo's my beat. If you think people are low, I wouldn't visit any gorillas for encouragement. The fur-bearing set may be genteel on the veldt, but in the dark piss-perfumed halls of Gotham, that country charm goes right out the window, or would if there were one. Some reporters might lobby for reform, but I've been covering this flea circus since Monstro was a pup, and believe me, sister, Danish modern would be wasted on them. Ideals and zoology don't mix. Sure, I used to write up the capybaras at play, any bilge for a byline, but once it sinks in that these are the world's largest rodents, your heart leaves the highlands. Cynical? Just the facts. Ma'am.

It was a typical morning in the Mammal House. Yesterday's school groups had deepened the salad of butts and Jujubes that carpeted the walkway, but in the dimness you could pretend it was the sticky moss of the forest floor, assuming you need to pretend in order to get through life. I was smoking a Camel—the carcinogen, not the ruminant—staking out a woodchuck my editor wants covered every February second. He must've had some night, because it was almost noon and his lettuce was turning brown without him. The woodchuck, not the editor.

I heard a seal bark down the hall, and a gust of chilly air rustled the litter briefly. Then I saw her—blonde, pert, Betty Co-ed in the Big City. She'd be the After in a beauty ad, but she was the Before of urban living. She squinted in the low light and had to feel her way along the guard rail to my side. The plaques that identify who's what are too grime-encrusted to read, but she gave this one a game stare. Finally she worked up her nerve and spoke to me.

"Excuse me, you don't happen to know what the animal is in this cage, do you?"

Her good manners killed me. "Do you need to know for school?" I said finally.

She swallowed but held on, trying to be chatty but twisting her little notepad like a schoolmarm in Injun territory. "Well you see I tried to read the label card but it's so dirty, I couldn't! It's the groundhog's cage I'm supposed to look for."

I let her get nervous, it was cute, and said, "Supposed to?"

"I'm a reporter." Shy, but proud. "I've just started with the *Clarion Chronicle Register* this week!"

I gave her the enigmatic smile I give unlikely prospects to save face. "Yeah? I hear they're about to fold. I'm with the *Times Star Blade*."

She couldn't conceal her surprise. "You are?" Then she couldn't conceal her guilt about not concealing her surprise. "I mean—uhh—So you're waiting to see if the groundhog comes out too?"

I lit another cigarette. "The zoo's my beat."

She was adorably unnerved. "I—uhh—I'm Dawn Anderson," she ventured. "I feel so silly, I even read up in the World Book on Groundhog's Day! It was originally Candlemas, the Purification of the Blessed Virgin."

I could've made hay out of that, but suddenly the door opened again and a shot of wind splashed my face. It was tinged with Scotch, a punk brand, too, and bore in a pudgy, unshaven clown in vintage breadline-wear. He hove toward us like a balloon in a Prohibition-Repealed parade.

"'S the groun'hog come out yet?" He wavered where he stood. "Sorry I'm late, I was at a bus plunge. Well, not *at*, but where it

was . . ." He blinked like a toad and recognized me. "Hey! How
are ya, Bix! They take you off the Sports Desk?"

"Not exactly, Hughie," I said in the cold voice I use to disas-
sociate myself from jerks when I'm with an unlikely prospect I'd
like to get likely with. "I sort of slid off, like you."

He missed the insult. "I'll say, what the hell kind of dumbbell
assignment is this? I don't mind human interest, a Mom Kills
Kids, Self—but who the—" He blinked again. "Who's this?"

She played tough, and shook his hand: "Dawn Anderson.
Clarion Chronicle Register."

"I'm Hughie of the *Ledger Sun Standard.*"

"Hughie's his first name," I explained. He was making me
look good. I remembered my bed wasn't made, but figured passion
would overlook sloppiness. "I see the *Ledger Sun Standard's* about
to go under," I smiled.

"And I see the *Times Star Blade's* about to fold," he offered,
trying to dismantle my charisma.

"Oh, can you still see, Hughie?" I said. Somewhere a cockatoo
cried. Things are tough all over.

She pointed into the cage, feeling bound to play hostess. "It
hasn't come out yet!" There was an awkward pause, the silence of
secret rivals, and she tried to make conversation. "You know, it's a
kind of *marmot! . . .*"

I ground out my cigarette. "I think it's asleep. Or scared."

She leaned over the rail and tried to draw the little marmot
out of hiding. We could see its concrete hutch outlined in a far
corner. She whistled and clucked, and threw in a few peanut
husks she found on the floor, but it had no effect on our quarry
and made me rethink our affair. She even clapped her hands a few
times, hoping to wake it, but she was as ineffectual as she was
intent.

Hughie was restless, as drunks often are. "Look, no one visits
the zoo on weekdays," he began. "Let's say he saw his shadow, no
more winter. Front page in a little box, real sweet."

It was an amoral suggestion. "Suits me," I said.

"Oh but, for one thing, don't you think we ought to just try real quick to get him to come out?" she stammered.

"They're nocturnal," I put in masterfully. "And there's no light in here for shadows anyway."

"But, also," she continued, though her voice was trailing off, "if he sees his shadow, it means *more* winter, not the end of winter . . ."

Hughie decided to take action, as drunks often do. He found a broom someone had left leaning on the rail and poked the handle end into the dark lair of the deadbeat, as if to rouse it. "Come on, you, up and at 'em, let's get this show on the road—"

She didn't go for that. "Do be careful!" she murmured. I don't like people who tell you to do be something. I decided she and I were through.

Hughie's jabs were getting violent and in his condition it made him sweat. Our cub reportrix was getting scared and her words of caution got high-pitched and gurgly, like a drowning mouse. I was reflecting on the ugliness of zoo life when Hughie suddenly stopped in mid-thrust. We heard a muffled woodland gasp.

"Um . . . found it," he said with ominous softness. "Or . . . its food dish, maybe." He gingerly lowered the broom handle to the cage floor, and tactfully let go, as if to minimize fingerprints. A squeamish pallor drained his round face, and he turned it to us helplessly, like a full moon in an Arctic sky. The cockatoo called again, distant and eerie.

She panicked and began to jabber hysterically. "No, like I said, if it sees its shadow it actually means there will be more winter. I know that sounds crazy, what with the sunshine, but it's true, or at least the true superstition!" It was a case of manic denial and I slapped her, hard.

"Shut up, honey," I said. I turned to Hughie, who was cowering like M in gangster court. "Influencing the news. That's a serious rap, Hughie." Humor always comes in handy in these situations. Then I took hold of both of them by their collars for a moment. *"He saw his shadow,"* I said significantly, and released them to consult my watch. *"When we left here at twelve fifteen . . . he had just seen his shadow and was in excellent health."* They stared at me. "Beat you to the pay phone," I added.

Hughie seemed to recover first. "Yeah!" he managed finally, and brightened. "He saw his shadow and we left! Anything could have happened then!" He took out a soiled handkerchief and ran it along the broomstick, though he had trouble dislodging it from inside the hutch. "Thanks, Bix, thanks," he murmured over and over. I hate him, but saving the day is a habit of mine, and women go for it. We stowed the broom in a utility closet with the zookeeper's empties and old scandal sheets.

A distinct buzzing of flies could be heard from the cage as we left. Miss Up-on-Marmots was faint with confusion and tailed us out of the place like a sleepwalking accomplice.

"Shouldn't we try to talk to someone about this?" she babbled. "What was it you said we should say happened? He saw his shadow? Or didn't he?" She stared ahead of herself like the crash survivors you find walking along interstates. She wandered away from us, finally. It was disillusioning, because I'd thought she was attractive. Still, I could have taken advantage of her. But I didn't. I'm no animal.

How Things That Don't Exist Work

No matter how much old people pretend to be amazed by how things have changed, science still can't keep pace with literature. A lot of fictitious inventions made workaday by a century of hack fantasy haven't yet come rolling off the assembly lines. All right— the giant television screen, they did come through on that one. But consider all these yet-to-be-invented states of being, all of them so easy to explain that a child can and often does.

INVISIBILITY

Everyone knows that *light rays can be bent around any object,* like superhighways around landmarks, and then resume their straight-and-narrow path as if nothing had ever gotten in their way. The resulting invisibility is obvious. Thus, if the object is human, the audience will see only a lectern and a pair of glasses floating in midair. Outer space is going to need a lot of spies, so let's get on the ball about applying this simple light-bending principle to trench coats and spacemobiles.

TELEPORTATION

Disassembling atomic structure and transmitting it in the form of energy to reassemble in a distant location is a notion far too familiar to rehash here. What we know is that it works. Still, millions fumble with subway tokens or get seasick on tramp steamers while this blessed nonexistent convenience lies fallow. We have enough diet drinks; let's turn our nimble-with-technology hands to the eternal human problem of getting to faraway places instantly.

TIME TRAVEL

A babe in arms can tell you the best method of entering the fourth dimension—just *go faster than light*. That's right: The minute you exceed the speed-of-light limit, you could find yourself in King Arthur's dungeon for the infraction. It isn't as if the fourth dimension were weird and undependable like the fifth or sixth dimension. Machines for time travel should be *the* upcoming tool of development in business; I bet Taras Bulba would really like to get his hands on a stapler or a Teflon pan. Back to the underground hangars, boys, and let's not come out till we're driving a stick-shift to Yesterday!

MINIATURIZATION

The ancients believed voodoo could reduce its victims to the size of ants, but now we know that to do that to victims or to anyone else requires *removing the space between the atoms*. The building blocks of all nature never come within miles of one another, figuratively speaking. There's enough space between the atoms of most people to shrink them clear out of sight, but why get ostentatious? All science needs to do is develop a remote control so nobody gets lost accidentally. Not much work remains except to think up a catchy phrase for the process, like "going doll."

FORCE FIELDS

Here the old "I am rubber, you are glue, bounces off me and sticks to you" principle prevails. All a force field has to do to protect you and yours is to *turn any incoming energy against itself.* All those antigravity devices work by the same inarguable law. With a little elbow grease down at the labs, mankind would never again have to use mud flaps on truck wheels. Smelly mosquito repellents would go the way of wolfbane, and football could get interesting again.

ROBOTS WITH ABERRANT PERSONALITIES

For all the hysteria about them, I've yet to see a computer go bucking down Main Street taking pot shots at frightened locals. Perhaps we aren't advanced enough yet to achieve accidentally the kind of fluke wiring that would create a psychotic machine, but accepting that attitude smells of defeatism. There must be plenty of ways to program a lively approach directly into a robot, there's no need to sit around and wait for an inadvertent cross-fusion of circuits to set the juggernaut in motion. Another advantage of crazed computers: Since they're inanimate, if they start foaming at the output slot, you can shoot them without compunction and still receive Communion on Sunday.

ANTIGRAVITY

Now, don't think that actual horseshoe-shaped, smartly striped magnets are involved here; that would be ridiculous. What we use is *antimagnetic drive.* All one has to do to escape gravity is to *negate it;* in even simpler terms, *reverse it.* Yet most of us, scientists included, seem willing to content ourselves with the crude, rudely interrupted fake freedom of a trampoline. Old Devil Gravity has tyrannized us—and me personally—for much longer than necessary. The future could use a little weightlessness.

My Sawdust Memories

Back in those days, a nickel bought you all the sawdust you could eat, and the butcher said "Thank you" when you bought it. The closest thing to a computer was the tiny abacus old Mr. Chang used in the back of that flooded basement Poppa rented to him, and we wanted nothing to do with it. We were all more innocent. I know my sister was, no matter what those unmarried head-shrinkers on TV might think.

Poppa was stern, the way no one troubles to be anymore. He allowed us to exhale only once a week, except on Thanksgiving, when we could breathe free all day, provided we did it in unison. People often comment on my enormous lung capacity, and I tell them I didn't get that strength from lazily gulping air like some harbor seal. As a birthday present, Poppa always used to remind us that "The bound grow straight." Not even zoos bother with that anymore—modern animals get whatever outlandish habitat their so-called hearts fancy. Indulging lions is not what preserves authority, I could tell anyone who'd ask, and animals don't even listen to my Poppa stories. I call that coddling the ignorant.

Of course, Momma balanced Poppa's strictness with her warm feminine weeping. On summer evenings, while Poppa was sanding the servants, she and those neighbor ladies who hadn't disgraced themselves for love would gather on our porch (cost, including swing, one dollar) and keen over the latest trifle overheard in town. God bless her, Poppa kept the Great War from her, so she had to cry about local horsewhippings or Irish workers pinned under fallen girders. Momma was as soft as a new-washed throw rug, and many's the flickering midnight nowadays that, as I watch these so-called ladies analyzing the news, I remember a simpler time when men were men and women took their word for it.

But it's a new world now. As much as my instincts warned me against doing so, when a foreclosure brought me to my hometown recently, I decided to drive with my doors locked to the old family place (initial cost, including spite fence and watchdog, fourteen dollars fifty cents) to see what the so-called passage of time had wrought. Where the exposed-wood shanties we playfully used to set afire had nestled, a terraced cement housing project loomed unflammably. As I edged my sedan cautiously past some rough-necking preschoolers, all of them inhaling and exhaling hell for leather (at least our unruly were cared for at home, in the secret room in the attic), I realized forlornly that their futuristic jungle gym stood where the neighborhood junk pile (all you could carry, free) had been. Where we had foraged and fought over carcasses were now only cold metallic bars and forgetful laughter. As for the house itself, the two unmarried ladies (conclude what you will) who now run it as a day care center have painted it sunshine yellow, a pathetic simulation of an ideal address that may fool dizzy working mothers, but not someone who remembers when the street was so exclusive only English-language records were allowed. Of course, radio ruined that.

"Miss," I asked one young supervisor who was trimming an obtrusive lilac bush. "Do you know who used to live here?"

"Nope," she answered.

"Nope?" I repeated drily, which should have shamed her.

"Nope," she persevered. "But it looked haunted till my boyfriend helped us paint it."

"Boyfriend?" I countered definitively.

"Excuse me, it's chocolate milk time."

At her age, I was forbidden to excuse myself, but in this dissolving day it's frowned upon to discipline other people's grown-up daughters, so I let her go, to feed children not her own and share love with a man she could not sue for divorce.

"This used to be a world that worked," I told a lounging moppet who had clambered onto a fender of my parked car and inserted a posy behind my windshield wiper. "Don't you have something disrespectful to say?" I added, apt and cutting humor to the oblivious being one of my strengths. The child shimmied from his perch and ran. What is it I long for so much, I wondered, as I got in my car and drove back to the airport.

When I got back to the city I reminisced to my wife about the visit. "Tell me," I said to her, "what is it I long for so much?"

"Silence," she suggested.

Now, silence isn't what I miss about childhood, I don't think, in fact I'm almost positive, but that's what she said, and she is my wife, so there may be something to it, there certainly is too much noise these days, though as I say, I don't know, I don't really know what she's talking about.

The Nine Imperfect Pups

Seven years ago last night, a wicked kennel club officer to the mighty ordered that a litter of nine imperfectly marked pups be destroyed. Their dam had been a distinguished breeder, but this was her last litter, and the pattern had faltered. A sympathetic underling, obsessed with guilt for having fatally overfed her goldfish in childhood, reported the pups drowned but secretly provided for their rearing in rural isolation. The pups grew up strong and beautiful, except for their imperfect markings.

Years passed. The sympathetic underling died of overeating, leaving the nine young dogs without sponsorship. Their drunken caretaker abandoned their country quarters, which were quickly overgrown. The dogs themselves disappeared, though there was none to mark their absence.

Last night, the kennel club officer, seven years more august and wicked, was about to be crowned king of the World Dog Show. The prodigious Consummatory Procession had just ascended the Dog Lovers' Sacred Vertiginous Altar when—a clatter from the rear! Ribbons rent! Exposed and peed on!

The dogs responsible have not been put to sleep. They managed to flee, their imperfect markings blending naturally with the crowd. An old, old bitch in the rear of the hall remembered, with a vague, difficult stirring, that years before, a litter of oddly spotted but to her beautiful pups had been spirited from her before their time. Even if she apprehended any connection between the two events, however, she could not offer to relieve the bafflement and sickened curiosity of the startled dignitaries as they beheld their avatar ravaged and drenched with urine. Dogs can't talk. Another cause hidden from history.

Profiles in Moolah

When Hobart Huntingbone Heitz died, on May 3, 1977, the New York Transportation Authority paid tribute to him by running all trains on time for a period of twelve hours. To observe mourning, the National Telephone and Telegraph System discontinued connecting all but its own calls for the next three days. Schoolchildren recited his name at assemblies, and Congress approved a farewell letter to him that is currently on display in the Library of Congress, since no one knew where to mail it.

Who was this man, that tycoons and tykes, that highbrows and hoboes alike felt his passing, as of a wind, sweeping across the gross national product? And who, if any, knew him well?

In many ways he was a man of contradictions, and in many ways he wasn't. His chief aide for years, Byron Wheeler, summed up his late employer in these words: "You're trying to trick me into saying something *crazy*, aren't you? I know how you guys operate. Get me to let something *wild* slip, you get it into the headlines, and pretty soon it's the class geek who gets stuck playing me in the school Current Events Pageant. No thanks, Mister Muckraking Inkslinger! Infamy I don't need. What was he like? Like a human being! There's human interest for you!"

This does little to dispel the clouds of mystery that surround Heitz and have, according to meteorologists, since 1946. Even the Heitz Gallery, a collection of his acquired paintings and statuary, has a Fifth Avenue address that no one has ever successfully lo-

cated, though photographs of its exterior occasionally surface in
Japanese magazines. The billionaire seemed to thrive on such secrecy, despite or perhaps to enhance his status as a popular leg-
end. His personal valet never spoke to him except via walkie-
talkie, and his own parents were fuzzy about the circumstances
of his birth.

As near as research can determine, however, Hobart Huntingbone Heitz was born of nameless and faceless immigrants on
New York's Lower East Side. (Perhaps it is the disadvantage of
facelessness that made it so difficult for his parents to discuss
him.) His patrician name bespeaks no Brahmin background, for it
is a composite of two of the neighborhood sweatshops and the deli
nearest his home at the time he was born. The year of Hobart's
birth is unknown, but he was still being carded in saloons as late
as 1919, so the date is conceded to be about 1895.

The Heitz household was neither gracious nor small; in addition to the nameless, faceless parents were a faceless sister, a
brother who was nameless, although he did have a face, and a
chauffeur who, although lacking an automobile, had ample face
and several names, the latter owing to a previous career outside
the law. Despite its bid for elegance (the chauffeur carried visitors
piggyback up and down the stairs of the five-flight walk-up), the
family was ragged, and one of them, though it's not clear which,
didn't smell very good. Hobart's mother had dreams of gentility
and refinement stemming from her once having looked at stereop-
ticon pictures of faraway places. She taught him to smoke cigarettes at an early age, in the hope that his stunted growth would
relieve the expense of new clothes. She was frail and birdlike and
spoke alternately in a southern and Irish accent. From her, Hobart
inherited an artistic spirit and a great love for her.

All that is known of Hobart's father is that he spent many
years as an immigrant laborer in the garment district, and that he
was the secretary of state under William Howard Taft. Beyond
that, all is mere conjecture, though much of the conjecture is

juicy and fascinating. In his memoirs (*None of Your Goddamn Business,* privately printed, 1972) Heitz does not mention his father and, indeed, mentions very little else. It is assumed this relationship with his father was quite painful, since it is not human nature to spare listeners the merely dull.

When it came time for the eldest son to be sent to school, Hobart's parents debated entrusting him either to Andover or Exeter, but finally settled on selling him to a children's workhouse closer to home. This proved too much for Hobart, and he ran away for good at age ten, taking only forged documents proving he was an orphan. Twelve blocks uptown, he traded his papers for a shovel and got a job digging basements for skyscrapers, which were just then coming into vogue. At night, he added to his meager earnings by hawking used matches outside the opera house. Both jobs were exhausting and brought little remuneration, but young Hobart, evincing a flair for the autobiographical that portended his eventual fame, stuck to the employment for over a year, comforted by the prospect of recounting his future past hardships.

One night in 1907, winter, the ersatz orphan was offering his preburned matches to sympathetic but resistant first-nighters at a production of *Aida*. Snow had fallen and a parked carriage near the stage door was skirted with snow. Since Hobart traveled everywhere with his shovel (he slept under it and used it to fry eggs over fires), he was enlisted to help clear the carriage wheels. After some digging, the notion was hit upon to use Hobart as a wedge to free the icebound wheels. His stunted size served the task well, and the carriage owner, Rhinestone Rob Grady, offered him a permanent position on his company staff. Hobart accepted.

Rhinestone Rob Grady was famous for his extravagant fur coats, his liberal gifts to beautiful women, and his fondness for overeating to the point of losing consciousness. He had made his money through profiteering, whatever that is, and by buying up all the air the railroads would have to pass through after everyone else had bought up the land. Whether he saw the young Heitz's

potential is unknown, but he always referred to his ward as "a
damn fine wedge."

Hobart moved into Grady's bachelor mansion, a rambling
structure on Madison, Park, and part of Lexington Avenue. He
was given a bath (this is where Part One of his memoirs ends) and
a new shovel. He was sent on errands when there wasn't much
work for him under the wheels, and he became a favorite of Rob's
Lower East Side tenants, who, according to a Grady press release
of the period, looked forward to rent day because "little Hobart"
was coming to collect.

Heitz departed from Grady in 1922 to set up his own business,
the venture that would culminate four decades later in the Heitz
Plaza in Chicago and thousands of branch offices here and abroad.
The novice businessman organized a firm that offered Orphan's
Insurance, a kind of protection children could purchase to provide
for themselves in the event of the sudden and untimely deaths of
those who provided for them. With a few friends, Heitz toured
local schoolyards, outlining the virtues of Orphan's Insurance to
attentive recess crowds. Eventually he added a mobile slide show
that graphically illustrated the sort of deaths that parents, especially careless or overtalkative parents, met every day.

Student involvement was great, and Juniors Security (his
name for the insurance) skyrocketed. In later years, Heitz was to
explain his motivation thus: "I was virtually an orphan. Naturally
I was moved by the plight of orphans, and felt all children should
be as well. Potential personal interest, of course, enlivens anyone's
sympathy."

The stock market crash ruined many businesses and certainly
put the kibosh on Thanksgiving in 1929. Economist K. G. Lister
has described the Depression as caused by "a bunch of guys all
spending money they didn't, you know, *have*." Heitz's business,
though shaken by the crash, survived it, and Heitz even collected
half a million dollars in damages by suing the Federal Reserve
Bank for mental cruelty. The nation's orphanages swelled, but

without adult guidance, no insured child had the legal know-how to collect from Heitz on his or her lost parents. Little Orphan Annie and Superman both made parentlessness seem fashionable, and more young people than ever bought coverage pending their possible waifdom.

Heitz himself, however, was increasingly dissatisfied with his venture. He complained that children were "immature" and announced he was seeking a business venture aimed at adults. He was forced to compromise, though, and organized an insurance foundation for actors. This move took him to Hollywood, where he began to produce films with Preston Von Piston, the acclaimed German director who had come to Los Angeles in 1930 to get oranges for a party but stayed to direct a talkie biography of Beethoven called *Thanks, Doctor Music*. The first movie Heitz produced for Von Piston was a World War I flying epic called (at Von Piston's insistence) *Wings, But Not Bird Wings, Man Wings*. Final title selection was an artistic luxury Heitz allowed Von Piston, a privilege the director enjoyed to the disadvantage of their next two collaborations, *Big Train Puffing Smoke Out* and *Woman Who Pretty*.

Though some critics admired Von Piston (James Agee praised his ability to hold a dollar in pennies in his mouth), his films were not commercial successes. The final movie Heitz produced was about a romance in a theater closed for repairs, and he himself chose the title *This Theater Is Closed for Repairs*. Again, customers seemed compelled to stay away. Heitz's Hollywood sojourn was not glorious.

It was in Hollywood, however, that he met his first wife, the actress and socialite Kitty FaSade. Kitty (whose real name was Doggy) had been considered to play the Air Force nurse in *Wings, But Not Bird Wings, Man Wings*, but lost her chance when Von Piston decided "women on the set were too distracting" and had all the female roles rendered through special effects. Heitz met her at a premiere party and playfully offered her money to sleep with him, and the romance was born. After a brief courtship (they went out to buy more ice) the two became man and wife, Heitz assuming the former role.

Kitty retired from the screen tests, and the couple moved to New York, where she began to develop her famous collection of classical and Renaissance sculpture that looked like her. Heitz returned to Juniors Security briefly, while planning his next move. He was a wealthy man at this time, but not yet wealthy beyond your wildest dreams.

He made several shrewd investments in 1939, most notably in vibrators, anticipating the World War II domestic market. He also bought a controlling interest in an adult insurance company and a used-car lot full of old Packards. This last purchase was to promote the greatest business innovation of his career, Motorists Mutual.

He hired several hundred skilled lawyers to drive the autos cross-country, causing accidents involving his own customers along the way. The lawyers made it look like the customers' fault, collected for it, and Motorists Mutual got back every premium it paid. Heitz was able by this ploy to raise the rates on customers who were proving "bad risks." And by bloating existing accident statistics, Heitz could justify generally higher rates for all his customers.

By 1950 Heitz was so well-to-do that Ripley's *Believe It or Not* ran several installments devoted exclusively to listing all the digits before the decimal point in his bank account. He incidentally acquired a corporation that subsequently skyrocketed, Food Technology—developers of Ultramilk and, eventually, Ultra-nonmilk. He was photographed in a bank vault for the cover of *Life*. Bob Hope told jokes about him. Kitty Heitz appeared regularly on the Ten Most Dressed List. Milton Berle told Bob Hope's jokes about him. It was at this time that Heitz had his nervous breakdown.

He and his wife as yet had no family, because Heitz was trying to figure out a way to have children, die, leave them their inheritance, and then somehow get it back. The couple did have a small staff that was kept blindfolded at all times so they would not be tempted to steal the valuable objects that decorated their home. Up to this time, though, he had displayed none of the secretiveness or eccentricities that would make him a national fascination in the sixties and seventies. He had not yet begun to speak only the first letter of the word he was thinking. He had not yet had his dogs arrested for conspiracy to evolve.

The first hint that there was any mental irregularity in the Sultan of Swag (as *Time* magazine dubbed him) was at a board meeting of Motorists Mutual in early 1953. In the middle of a discussion of potential expansion into maritime mishaps, Heitz asked his employees to remove their faces and show him their brains. Heitz repeated his request, and after a brief silence the uncomfortable staff began tugging at their faces as if to unbutton them. Following some spirited grunts and some bravura staging (one particularly ambitious junior partner closed a window on his head to suggest he would uncork it), Heitz's underlings looked to him again, hoping this simulation would satisfy him. Their employer surveyed them with disgust and muttered, "You didn't really try."

Alerted that their superior was entertaining crotchets, his workers expressed their alarm by being more sycophantic and agreeable than ever. The following week, Heitz addressed a large body of reporters who had come to eat his buffet lunch and suspect his motives. After some apparently harmless introductory remarks about how American Indians didn't have to shave and how ancient a beast the opossum is, Heitz's comments became unusual and disjointed. He divided the assembly into halves and attempted to direct them in a contrapuntal version of "Roll Me Over in the Clover."

A murmur rustled through the crowd, and one radio newsman asked Heitz why he had summoned the press to so unorthodox a free meal. Gripping the lectern and swaying visibly, the great figure answered in words that have become a household joke in most Wall Street offices: "Because, Mister Dudley, God has loaned the world to his teenage son, and we'd better get ready for the smashup." Heitz then lost consciousness and was rushed to the Thompson Clinic for Needless Expense in nearby Evanston. Here he was elaborately tested and so billed for such discomforts as bullet wounds, paper cuts, cat bites, and rapture of the deep. Doctors X-rayed him extensively and even traced his body on tagboard with colored pencils. No possible expense was avoided to determine his condition. He had been reduced to the world's third richest man before the medical profession was satisfied that he had suffered a nervous breakdown and not, in fact, frostbite. Meanwhile, the press had exploited the incident by playing up Heitz's sacrilege, and the *Daily News* proclaimed MILLIONAIRE CLAIMS TO KNOW GOD'S PLANS. The National Council of Churches met to discuss returning the five million dollars Heitz had given them a month earlier, and finally resolved instead to maintain an icy silence on the subject.

After a week of sedation, Heitz was dismissed to the care of his personal servants. Once in his own bed, he resumed control of his business, which had been supervised in his seven-day absence by a succession of vice-presidents, each of whom had shot his predecessor and enjoyed a few heady hours in office. (The phone bills these interim leaders had piled up later proved to be the single greatest operating expense in Heitz's career.) Kitty returned from Acapulco, where she had gone to pray for her husband's recovery, tanned and ready to serve him. To assist her in this service she brought back with her three Mexican youths in the first brown blush of manhood.

Heitz continued to oversee all his corporation's interests, and for reference used toy Civil War soldiers spread on his blankets to represent the various departments and factions under his control. Kitty, careful to avoid the contagion some associate with nervous breakdowns, kept herself and the three Mexican youths protectively confined in the guest house behind the mansion.

In March of 1954, Heitz returned to his offices but lasted only three weeks. Complaining about the ventilation one day, he supposedly remarked to his aide Byron Wheeler, "Any damn thing could come buzzing out of those air vents—tsetse flies, gnats, cicadas. It's distracting." The office atmosphere became strained by his insistence on affecting a beekeeper's outfit at all times.

There was no real need for him to go back to work. He had more money than he and an expressly hired staff of imaginative people knew what to do with. Finally, the second breakdown, long feared by those who did not stand to profit by it, necessitated Heitz's discreet abdication from regular involvement in the affairs of the companies he owned.

Testifying for a Senate committee that April, he denounced Communists with what newsmen called "a provocative dance" and fled to the lap of the Lincoln Memorial, where he named a lost Boy Scout his heir. Twelve-year-old Tyro Novak was disqualified a day later, when it was learned his parents were foreigners with glasses.

The medical and journalistic worlds returned their attention to Heitz, and once again he proved a lucrative enigma for both. He was flown back to New York, where he entered a private clinic along with his wife, who was under treatment for lockjaw. One surgeon suggested "a broken heart" as the cause of the billionaire's troubles, but, though widely praised by critics, the theory was ultimately rejected. Heitz himself seemed to link his idiosyncrasies with his hard-won wealth. "I seem crazy because I'm the only man on earth who doesn't need to impress anybody. I'm not overtired, I'm overrelaxed," he wrote in a letter to fourteen-year-old Mimi Gillis, notifying her that she had been chosen at random from the Milwaukee high school register to be his successor.

While resting at the clinic, he began working on his memoirs, though his love for secrecy was such that even sixteen years later all his publishers had to show the public was five hundred pages of erasures. Mimi Gillis was flown to the New York offices and

tutored in accounting while Heitz arranged for an official passing-
the-crown ceremony in the New York Stock Exchange. Though
confined to his room, he spent hours writing telegrams every day
and communicated with his aides by flipping the Venetian blinds
in code. When a complicated office intrigue required Mimi to go
away to have a baby, he was depressed by the delay and promptly
chose another potentially promising unknown from the records of
the Des Moines public schools, this time a hyperactive child with
a history of arson. Timmy Frayne was the youngest ever ordained
as Heitz's successor (ten), but Heitz, aware that he could never
return to the helm, rushed his protégé through a combined course
on table manners and great Civil War strategies. Timmy received
the mantle of leadership at the gala Wall Street ceremony originally intended for Tyro or Mimi, on July 19, 1954. The business
has flourished unprecedentedly in the three decades since his
accession.

Heitz was now free to become as squirrelly as he pleased. His
divorce from Kitty shocked the social world (or at least it looked
shocked), but he generously granted her possession of all the objects in the house that looked like her. Her own autobiography,
Pile Your Plate, There's No Second Helpings, offers this insight into
their separation:

> The lawyer came to visit us with his little black bag, and be-
> cause we hated each other so much, God gave us a beautiful
> tiny divorce out of that hate. And that's where divorce comes
> from.

Slowly the famous Heitz preoccupation with his own bodily
functions began to manifest itself. The hygienic urge that had
prompted him to don beekeeping togs now flourished in his soli-
tude and self-absorption. He hired a squad of artists to render their
conceptions of various vistas of the inside of his body. Most of
these remain in litigation with the rest of the estate, but one, *The*

Lungs at Twilight, can be seen in the lobby of the Heitz Plaza in Chicago.

His concern about bacterial infection grew so morbid that he refused to eat anything that had been inside his mouth. He married porn star Needa Jones and specified, though they were never to meet, that her films be shown only to him. His paranoia proliferated. In November of 1966 he became convinced that his two German shepherd guard dogs, Dutch and Frieda, were secretly attempting to evolve to a more intelligent species and thereby take over the Heitz operations. The dogs were arrested and held on suspicion for "a period not to exceed eighty million years" in order for the local police department to see if there was any evidence supporting the billionaire's "willful evolution" charge. The dogs died in captivity without issue, and the charges were dropped.

In March of 1977 the federal agents assigned to sifting through Heitz's garbage contracted trichinosis, prompting the government to suspend surveillance activities until a hardier strain of G-man could be developed. At the time of the suspension, records show that whoever was living inside the Heitz mansion was eating exclusively Chinese take-out food and Easter candy. Airplane parts and secondhand cyclotrons were also noted in the estate's trash cans, causing some speculation that Heitz was considering personal military expansion. Following the confusion wrought by the trichinosis tragedy, Heitz's activities were shrouded in mystery until official word of his death came on June 5, 1977.

He was found in the tub, where he had been abandoned because the staff assumed he was an effigy in a beekeeper's coat. The autopsy was conducted on Prugh Bottleman, Heitz's public relations director, since the tycoon had specified in his will that his body was to be examined only by proxy. The coroner ruled that according to his evidence, Heitz had been dead for ten to fifteen years, but admitted that "it might be the aftershave he was wearing" that gave that effect.

The enigmatic figure's ashes were scattered to the winds

a week later, frustrating some who said they would dance on his grave, although one intrepid adversary attempted to skydive through his smoke as it rose from the crematorium. The will was simple. Kitty and Needa received autographed pictures of each other; Byron Wheeler was given "any perishables whatsoever that remain in the house, including flowers." One million dollars was allocated to the Society for the Promotion of Perpendicular Interment (he had always wished to conserve space), and the remainder of his one-and-a-half-billion-dollar estate was distributed evenly among four schoolchildren in Santa Fe, New Mexico, who had been chosen at random about a year earlier. It was later learned that Heitz rewrote his will every six months, always inserting the names of different arbitrarily determined youngsters, and always changing the selection when any of them reached the age of fifteen.

"Maybe it was his way of saying thanks to all the children who bought Orphan's Insurance in the thirties," offers Jared Weinstock, whose life work has been a biography of Harriet Beecher Stowe. "Children seemed to play an important role in his life, though I don't know. Little Eva, now there was a child."

"His life wasn't exactly his statement," said newsman Wiley Maudlin the day after Heitz's death. "It was more of an utterance, really, a pronouncement, an assertion, that's it, a declarative assertion. To me anyway."

Heitz's mystery is America's legacy. The perplexity re-echoes off Time's sheer canyon walls, but no answer answers.

The Platonic Cube

This is it, or would be: the icy, inarguable essence. We can see it perfectly, but we can't find it. It is absolute and elsewhere, the unvisible, irreal, and final authority. It's clean, free of demeaning color and location, and epitomizes three-dimensionality without taking up space. It has no shadow, because it is lit on all sides with the even sourceless light of nowhere. There is no air to dim it with haze or wind to shake it. More like a figure on a page than a figure on a page is, it has no true size. It is all sizes. Not even atoms could align this scientifically: every angle is right enough to skewer a mote, but of course no dust specks are allowed. Yes, this would be it, so it must be. Perfect, for once: lines speeding soundlessly to their vertices, planes convening seamlessly, eternally becalmed, reflecting on all sides the emptiness that surrounds ideal states, the intentionless glow, the strict hush, the diamond-crisp exactitude more patient than diamond, the stately unavailability and unavailingness of truth.

The Earth Hour

NASA engineers have placed gold-plated long-playing records of human sounds aboard Voyager I and Voyager II in a project they have called "Greetings from Earth."

National Aeronautics and
Space Administration
Washington, D.C.

Gentlemen:

Human music—I am with you all the way. But let's hope we're being honest about ourselves to alien beings. We're not touching up the little ol' resumé on these records, are we? Don't get me wrong—Bach may be our mightiest self-recommendation, but those onion-headed prodigies out Orion way might be more astounded by our actual banality! Look, give *me* funding; here's the Top Ten program I'll line up for the Earth Hour:

1. *"Chopsticks"*

Its charisma is limited, no matter how jazzy the arrangement, but although there's fancier music, there's none so honest: "Chopsticks" is the ABC of mortal exertion. It's such a weird introduction to us, or to anything, that I think those eavesdropping unimaginables would just have to keep listening.

2. *"Happy Birthday"*

Now that we've got their attention, let's hit 'em broadside with our theme song. Not classy but, you'll agree, very Earth. All that clangorous, foggy getting-together at parties in anticipation of free cake. If linear time has any meaning to them, the pathos of this limp anthem to its onslaught will set their feelers aquiver.

3. *"Nyaa-Nyaa-Nya-Nyaa-Nyaa"*

True, it's not strictly music, but what is? Besides, they don't know about the distinctions we make; they might not tell cricket sounds from dance music. Sending this brief recitativo might risk interplanetary warfare, but at least they'll realize that we're not 100 percent water, and that it's not good manners that got us up from the lobe-finned fishes. They might as well know that rudeness is the way on this vicious, nearly spherical cafeteria. Anyhow, I for one am willing to put up with the nuisance of interplanetary warfare just to get a look at these yoskies once and for all.

4. and 5. *"I've Been Working on the Railroad"*

Is it honest? No, not exactly, especially since most of the people who have sung it have never worked on any railroad. But, remember, we want to be honest even about our dishonesty; this way they'll know that whether or not we work hard, we pretend to like it. The progress of this tune will give them a whiff of progress in general. The song never ends; it has successively merrier and more uncalled-for extensions, like a house whose senile owner is always adding lean-tos. After Dinah and her horn, there is a crazed shift to the kitchen and, finally, a free-for-all of "fee-fi-fiddli-i-ohs"—God knows what's happened to the railroad. If Manifest Destiny has a musical spokesman, this is it.

6. *"Body and Soul"*

After that last one, we'll need sympathy fast. Biology has victims too. "For you I sigh, for you, dear, only . . ." Sharing heartbreak with strangers may not be polite, but maybe they'll be flattered that we confide in them. After all, we *are* Mother Earth; all the tourist billboards say TRY OUR FAMOUS FEELINGS! And, luckily, this kind of music can make even our most psychotic depressions seem sexy. Charlie Mars may not dig torch music, but even if he can't scan the blues, he might just get agitated enough to want to know if the guy and girl ever get back together, and contact us.

7. *"The Pachelbel Canon"*
I know I cut Bach out of town, but this piece is short and serene, which will surprise them after what they've heard so far. And when they check in to tell us how much they like the Pachelbel, we can shrug and say, "You should hear our *big* composers!"

8. *"The Loco Motion"*
This tells them how we get around.

9. *"Holiday for Strings"*
I think those Other Worlders are ready for some more complicated social patterns. This industrial cheer-maker, the granddaddy of Muzak, is the best melodic equivalent we could choose of mannered behavior, apparently benign institutions, and self-presentation of all sorts. This piece isn't personal, it isn't impersonal—what the heck is it? If I know those extragalactic intelligences, they'll put z and z + 1 together and realize that we can conceal ourselves from them and from one another and still pretend we're out in the open. Intrigue like that should be tantalizing.

10. *"Ol' Man River"*
Sure, I'd rather close with a tasteful string quartet, but the finale has to be straightforward enough to appeal to some gigantic amphibious protozoan a thousand parsecs thataway. Interpretation is going to be crucial here, so let's get a version that really lets 'er rip—no youth choirs need apply. Keep the violin arrangement

in check, no hotdogging on the closing phrases, and there won't
be a dry eye in the sky.

Of course, the arts councils will show up on our isolated record-
ing-studio doorstep with shopping bags full of Verdi cassettes, and
they'll point out that we could do a lot better for those silvery
heathens than piping them hokey popular tunes. Yes. But let's not
be importunate. Superciliousness is not going to bring them call-
ing with bonbons and a cure for cancer. Do you think they want
edification lessons from us, countlessly distant as we are and still
molten at our core? Let's take our cue from all those teen dating
manuals: To Make Friends, Be Yourself.

April First Is the Cruelest Day

In a thousand straight-faced households this morning, there's sugar in the salt shaker and grease on the bathroom doorknob. Sidewalks near veterans' homes glitter with glued-down quarters. Children point out monsters behind their playmates, and the office live wire has posted bulletins of dismissal for all his co-workers. This temporary abandonment of our higher primate integrity could be attributed to what the poet calls "you know, *spring*," or even to the imminent income tax, but any schoolboy will tell you: "Are you for real? It's April Fool's Day. Moron."

This isn't the truth, of course. It's actually Christmas today, not April Fool's at all. Noel Noel. Where does the time go? No, just joshing. It is April Fool's Day. It is. But if bland and momentary mischief is the sum of this day's thrills, why do problem children and hired hands everywhere so look forward to it? Moreover, why do the oppressed stop at a raw egg on the boss's chair? What keeps this free-for-all so tepid? What, when all is sprayed and dumped, *is* April Fool's? Who is this Shriner in the senate of our days, this gate-crasher at the calendar's celebrity roundup?

It isn't even a holiday, exactly, not any more than Senior Grub Day or the first day of duck-hunting season, anyway. We could examine its origins by poring over old Georgian records and crumbling broadsides, but why give it that satisfaction? It's a day for the attention-hungry as it is. However, we do know—at least, I do—that centuries ago the New Year was celebrated in late March to coincide with the vernal equinox (a Druidic feast that eventually developed into the Academy Awards), until someone pointed out that the New Year actually began in January. Without television, there had been no widespread awareness of year-end sales to clue people in to their error. The adjustment was made in the calendar, but some medieval diehards were loath to reschedule the caterers, so they had their party in April anyway. They were referred to as "April Fools," but you can bet that those who referred to them that way still showed up at the party. After a while, this tradition of playful deception entitled merrymakers to wander the streets with long sticks and hit at each other while denying they were doing so. Some scholars believe this is when the shift from chivalric to modern romance took place. Finally, the parties themselves died out, but the foolish behavior continued, a phenomenon comparable to politics after an election.

Over the years, a repertoire of standard pranks accumulated, like an unwritten alternative to the "Oxford Book of Carols." It is said that Sir Walter Raleigh devised the ploy of inquiring for himself in cans at tobacconists, only then gigglingly to demand his own release. The classic "hotfoot," a favorite of the barracks and the cartoon screen, most likely originated in Florence at the fertile time when both leather shoes and sulfur-tipped matches were being perfected. Another timeless inpertinence, the bucket-of-water-balanced-above-doorway, may have come from as remote a source as the pubs of the Aran Islands, where missionaries could find no straightforward way to get the natives near the baptismal water. During the days before telephones, crank calls were pioneered by drunken town criers ("Winged snakes, but otherwise all is well") and the rare whimsical Indian who fudged his smoke signals just for a mini-ha-ha. Do not suspect that this may not be true.

Now that being funny is as obligatory in America as being honest was in many now-vanished societies, the first of April is a field day of hemi-semi-demi-anti-establishment-from-within pranks, a festival of idly cruel behavior to match the new clothing styles. Young professionals parade their closeted anarchistic urges as if they were Easter bonnets (e.g., answering the credit department phone with "City Morgue"), but, like the carnival or the weather, April Fool's in its glory is a rural and puerile event only. It requires the infant savagery that also builds kissing booths. A toy bazooka firing flour may be blatant, but it does take responsibility for itself. What's unusual and comforting about this day isn't the crazed little deceits, it's the gleeful honesty with which they're announced afterward. Whatever Pan's failings, he's no liar.

A joy-buzzer makes contact, after all, and your first boyfriend only dipped your pigtail in the inkwell, he didn't set it on fire. Pranks are the stutterings of love. Honest. Have a chocolate. They only smell like soap, they're really good. Go ahead.

Top Opening Lines

Sooner or later the chemical chains that add up to you are going to start militating for maximum expansion, and when they do, you're going to think it's love you're after. Sadly, the much criticized complexity of life makes assurance of true and furthermore available love unlikely without conversation first, so brace yourself for some of the symbolic higher-primate exchanges that have made man sweep the honors in *Bartlett's Familiar Quotations*.

Unless you're a lawyer, though, you can't force anyone to talk to you, and even then, the talk might seem strained. Therefore, some Open Sesame or verbal pageboy is needed that will dispose your object to receive you, although the time-proven candidates for First Line are depressingly if purposefully unmagical. Intensely conservative as our chemical chains are, they like to sight solidity before lowering the landing gear, so regardless of the cute ripostes that are meat and drink to underage checkout girls and James Bond, it's the plain, even the wan phrases that excel in actual highway tests.

Here are the five most lusterless and qualified choices for Opening Line, one of which just may be the appropriate salvo for your next targeted dreamboat.

1. *"Hello."*
The Tiffany of greetings, this elegant little black word commits you fully to your prospect without in any way limiting the

scope of what's to come. Studies have shown that your quarry is likely to match your hello, however reluctantly; then, of course, you must start from zero again, but you've "opened Japan," as historians say, and it's now a relationship, even if they turn away coldly. After all, now it's *you* they're avoiding, and only seconds before you were mere strangers.

When inflecting this word, avoid the musical comedy "va-va-voom" subtext, however much you wish to fly your enthusiasm's colors. You may mean "My astral mate at last!" but it'll read as "I see supper!" Also, "*Hi*" is a tolerable sleeveless variant, but under no circumstances use "*Yes!*" on its own.

2. "*My name's ——.*"

This sacrifices both mystery and coyness immediately, but it does show a certain forthrightness, even a compulsion to confess that many associate with intimacy. Its openness (he or she could go right to the police with the information, after all) obliges anyone honorable to offer up his or her own name, and, by primitive superstition, his or her very soul, in response.

If your name is Crusher or Pee Wee, it may be a provocative general introduction to you, and in any case, your partner can always get the chat, and destiny, rolling by saying, say, "Gina? Oh, are you Italian?"

Again, watch inflection, or your intended may suspect you're seizing a narcissistic opportunity to recite your own name, especially if you include any roman numerals that may follow it. So offer your name factually, like a placard at the zoo. Curiosity is most likely to explore in safety.

3a. "*Are you a model/dancer/Swedish?*"

Only the stupid will be fetched by this superficial tribute, though you'd be surprised what a long-standing good time many stupid people can show you. As vulgar come-ons go, this one's pretty subtle—it's even phrased passively, as a question. The lesser, old-school variant, "*You look like a great painting*," might lead to schoolyard Picasso jokes, or worse, classroom discussion. Comparisons to flowers and deities provoke prickly unease in these literal times, and old boyfriend/old girlfriend analogies unnerve even an eager subject. Perfectly objective observations like "*My mother had a pin like that*" land somewhere uncomfortably between the Gothic and the Platonic. Specific praise seems fetishistic, so again, generality is the ticket: Let them make their own sundae.

3b. "*I just want you to know you're beautiful.*"

As modestly winning as it may seem, this oil-tinged zephyr doesn't quite sell the way you would think. Though a saintly way to mash, it lacks the promise of Question Form, and though we love to hear ourselves say it, the selfless compliment always engenders suspicion in the recipient. There is, of course, the pathetic implication that, having delivered your gift horse, you will now slip into the gloaming, so if you don't poignantly vanish, your motives will begin to smell up the romantic glen you've evoked. If ever, this "socko" approach is serviceable for those rare right-before-getting-off-the-subway moments; at least you might run into the beauty concerned another day, premoistened for second-level blandishments. Needless to say, your chemical chains hate high-risk long-term sallies like this.

4. "*May I ask the time?*"

Though one of the top five, this one is still very bad. It exploits and dismisses the beloved before you've even been introduced, although you might think it's an ingenious way to have the two of you thrown together by business matters. True, it obliges the Watched to converse with you, but it implies you have interests elsewhere, or are restless where you are, or (if it's late) that both of you should be in bed, a hasty and finally defeatist argument for togetherness. Still, mechanistic as it is, it beats the unduly solic-

itous "*Are you having a good time?*" As for "*Do you come here
often?*"—its inquest into a stranger's figurative virginity lacks
even camp potential to excuse it, except perhaps on a Nobel Prize
dais, and even then there's a likely language barrier.

5. "*Excuse me—Don't I know you?*"

This is the closest to magical of all because it attempts to by-
pass completely the problem of speaking to someone for the first
time, by pretending that in fact you've already done so and can
now just relax and try to remember each other. It can be followed
with a quick rifling-of-the-past using whatever you perceive to be
your best credentials: "The Winter Olympics? Northwestern? The
Small Boat Show?" People doubt their own memory, and even if
your fascinator demurs, you can coast into Where-or-When meta-
physics with "Well, it *feels* as if I know you." The Reachable Rose
may incline its head into some other warm wind, but you'll have
the consolation that anyone who'd spurn an old friend isn't good
enough for your chemical chains anyhow.

Well, there they are—admittedly an unprepossessing clutch of
phrases, especially when prepossessing is the goal—but, if you
think flippancies like "*Which way to the frozen yak?*" will disarm
a fellow shopper, you've been reading too many quack guides to
sensuality. Also, as a last warning, contentions of inferior drama
aside, beware of the spirited wrangle that you plan to turn to passion. If you challenge a prospect with "*Do you really eat that
junk?*" or "*What are you so smug about?*" don't expect the scuffle
that follows to melt into a helpless embrace. No, let your spoken
emissaries be drably dressed to imply great wealth. Begin with an
aura of effortless health. Dupe them with a competent phenotype.
Let their chains think yours are less hysterical than they are. It's
high time you fooled nature for once.

Insert Title Here

(*Lord Dessington's well-appointed study. There is a door at right leading to the reception room and a fireplace whose mantel is cluttered with the paraphernalia of a life spent in the Far East. Lord Dessington enters in a smoking jacket. He is a portly, diffident man, nearing old age. He opens the windows that lead to the terrace and takes a deep breath*).

LORD DESSINGTON: An immediately gripping opening line.
(*Enter Liesl, the maid*)
LIESL: Perfunctory response?
LORD DESSINGTON: Just as good a second line.
LIESL: Whatever comeback you think best.
LORD DESSINGTON: I start to say something when—(*He is interrupted by a loud knock at the door*)
VOICE (*urgently, offstage*): An intrusion of some sort!
LORD DESSINGTON: Whatever line you like here.
LIESL: And here, though something doesn't sound right.
(*Enter James March, a handsome young attorney*)
MARCH: Something no doubt rather complicated.
LORD DESSINGTON AND LIESL (*together*): We respond.
MARCH: Then further details.
LORD DESSINGTON: Additional response, if you like.
MARCH: Further dialogue if absolutely necessary, but something should happen now.

LIESL (*after a tense pause*): Another line.

(*Lord Dessington and March react with shock. Two policemen enter and lead Liesl away in handcuffs*)

LIESL: An exit line of some description. (*She is gone*)

MARCH (*lighting a cigarette*): I set you up for your last line.

LORD DESSINGTON (*serenely*): My last line.

(*Curtain, if that's what you want*)

Shop

Building the Bomb on a Budget

To paraphrase the very smart Albert Einstein, "Things cannot be made simpler than they are." This inconvenient truth has curbed many a would-be nuclear potentate whose intellect was incommensurate with his appetite. Even though the publication of hydrogen bomb plans was widely anticipated by disgruntled would-haves everywhere, the instructions for fusion offered were too complicated for the average basement and intellect that works there. Truth, sadly, does not have falsehood's luxury of absolute clarity.

Aptitude and achievement need no longer be related, however. At the expense of a few frills like a speedometer or a reusable canister, you can build a simple but sincere *fission* bomb at home for a fraction of what it would cost to have a full-fledged fusion bomb catered.

First, wash your hands. A little stray grit or margarine in your hairbreadth mechanisms and you may find yourself festooning several miles of nearby woodland. Next, put the dog in the playroom to keep him from getting underfoot later. Now, let's review the basic building blocks of the universe.

All matter is composed of atoms, particles so small they cannot be purchased individually. Look at your hand: What you're seeing is trillions of atoms traveling in what is called "hand formation." You will see a similar effect on your other hand and, to a lesser extent, on your feet.

Some matter is not quite as blessed with perimeters as you. Gases, for instance, often seem invisible—at least the good ones do—and yet they fully qualify as matter and even get the run of most planets. The important thing to remember is that *matter can be neither created nor destroyed,* though it can get very discouraged. Sometimes it can *look* destroyed (the "smithereens" effect), but it has merely been *redistributed* from here to kingdom come.

A nuclear bomb simulates destruction better than anything else going. Its enormous energy is released by tampering with atoms. This process is so complicated that many people become artists to avoid thinking about it. The stars in the sky, for example, are all huge, continually exploding natural hydrogen bombs, a fact songwriters never mention.

Whatever you do, don't confuse *fusion* with *fission. Fusion,* also called the "caramel corn" syndrome, occurs when atoms of a light element are heated to the point at which they fuse into a single larger element. Hydrogen (a particularly airy one), for instance, produces helium, anticlimactically enough. Conversely, *fission* occurs when a jumbo atom like uranium (which, to give it credit, moves very gracefully for its size) is split into smaller atoms that can then be fenced without raising international suspicion. Usually, however, the heat and energy released cause more atom-splitting and whizzing neutrons, starting an uncontrollable chain reaction that makes for world power and preferred seating at better restaurants. Since fission is the opposite of fusion, this sequence of unstoppable explosions can also be called *confusion.*

Now then, check on the dog to make sure it isn't tearing up the floor pillows. Wash your hands again if you touched the dog and return to the project site. To start with, be sure you have strong overhead light to avoid eyestrain on the detail work. Now clear away stray tools and be on the lookout for Uranium 235, which may be hard to get if you don't have connections. Uranium 235 is an *isotope* of ordinary uranium, which means that it looks and acts like it's normal, but after a while you wake up and realize you've been living with a stranger. What's worse, U^{235} (as friends call it) cannot be coaxed from its constant and, for our purposes, worthless companion, U^{238}, by any chemical means, and that includes alcohol. Physical means must be utilized, if you get my drift.

Shaken vigorously enough, your kitchen sieve can be used to "sift" the two strains apart. By and by, you will have a sizable mass of fissionable material. This is called the atomic "pile," or "mound." Keep it loosely packed—Pressure, be forewarned, is just the sort of thing that elevates a bomb from uncritical to critical mass. Some people claim that "critical mass" refers to Luther's first Protestant service (these punsters should figure high on your hit list once the bomb is finished), but in fact critical mass is the bingo point that lets slip your mushroom-shaped genie. A juicer or a hamburger press, with certain modifications such as dynamite, can be used to induce critical mass.

Pat the atomic mound into a generous, hollow sphere and frost it with conventional high explosives before canning. The bomb's outer case may look drab and metallic, so feel free to enliven it with colorful decals and graffiti like "Here Comes the Cavalry" or "From Kate Smith with Love." Bear in mind, of course, that your nuclear bomb will perforce be an experience for all ages, so moderate your decorations for family viewing.

There you have it. If money talks, an atomic bomb sings opera. You'll probably want to save your handiwork for a while before using it, or shop for a surplus B-52 to go with it. However, while you bask in the glow of your accomplishment (and any stray uranium), try to bear your new influence graciously. Keep yourself well-groomed, chew with your mouth closed, and express interest in your visitors' favorite sports and hobbies. No one likes a "show-off" nuclear power, and while it's true that you can now make anyone you want dance with you, yours won't be true popularity until the neighbors say, "Henry, if anyone had to have the bomb, *I'm glad it was you.* Here's my weekly cash tribute."

Aunt Buddy's Christmas Gifts

to Make at Home for Less Than Something Good Would Cost

Chances are you can't afford to give anything like good Christmas presents to your loved ones, or, in case you're Protestant, your liked ones. Of course you could give everyone those old-standby fingernail clippers that are always handy and always getting lost, but why give a meager useful gift when large useless ones are less expensive and win more Dutiful Affection points? Here are a few stocking-stuffers you can make from things found around your home, and if you're daring as well as hard-up, remember they're found around other people's homes, too, if you get my meaning.

TRAVEL-AT-HOME GLASSES

It's hard to find new uses for old prescription eyeglasses, but this is definitely a use, in a playful sort of way. Take the old eyeglasses and paste inside the lenses pretty landscape scenes torn from magazines. If you have two copies of the same magazine, the scenes could match, but they don't have to. Now your invalid friend can "travel" to lovely places in his or her own sickbed!

WATERPROOF OBJECTS

Anything that isn't traditionally waterproof can be made so, just by coating it completely in Scotch tape. Old hockey caps, scrapbooks, and even favorite plush toys take on a new sheen, and incidentally become great accessories for a walk in the rain. Remember to leave airholes for living things!

LIGHTBULB COVERS

Many people worry about breaking spare light bulbs, since the shards are so tiny and insidious. Old mittens with the thumbs cut off and the holes sewn up make excellent lightbulb covers. Some people like these so much they even keep burned-out bulbs in them! One decorating suggestion: Knit a little hook onto the mittens and they can hang in a row like Christmas stockings or utensils, a fond but functional addition to any kitchen or study. They aren't a good idea for bulbs already in use, since they obscure light and cause fires.

CHRISTMAS CARD FIREPROOFING

It's hard to keep every Christmas card you ever received because, left unattended, piles of them tend to catch on fire. Write a note to your friend volunteering your time some weekend to come over and go through his or her house and spray fireproofing on any and all Christmas cards. Scotch tape is a dependable inexpensive alternative. Someday you two can compare collections!

A WASTEBASKET FOR DREAMS

Got an old unused wastebasket? I have dozens, and this whimsical gift softens hearts as water does white bread. Take one of your old unused wastebaskets and cover its outside with pleasing scenes torn from magazines or, if you want to make a production out of it, add seashells, dry macaroni, or glitter. Across the top of the receptacle, fasten a net (old mesh pantyhose can be cut up for this purpose) that "saves" any dreams that might be thrown into it, so the owner never really "throws away" any old dreams forever. A beautiful thought, and because of its size, it seems like a big gift! Better write "Wastebasket for Dreams" on it, though, because a lot of people don't get it right away. Also, remind your friend not to use it as a real wastebasket, because crumpled papers bounce out of it and cause fires if the wiring is bad.

HOT WATER BOTTLE PURSE

All you need is a cord or shoelace added as a strap, and this fire-resistant red rubber beauty is ready to go! Before you give this gift, be sure to find out if your friend has any wide or long objects, since only very skinny and small ones can go in an empty hot water bottle and come out again too. Marbles are perfect for storing in this purse, although it gets a little heavy for older ladies. And better write "not for hot water" on it to avoid accidental destruction of crucial papers.

CANNONBALL CENTERPIECE

As souvenirs of Civil War memorials I've visited, I naturally have a large collection of old cannonballs, even a few bronzed ones. I don't need all of them, so sometimes I cover one with attractive couples torn from magazine advertisements, or old seed packet covers. It's also a peerless paperweight for a sturdy desk or vanity, and reminds us of the verdict of history.

PAPER BAG HOLDER

Above cupboards and under sinks are no places for valuable brown-paper bags. A medium-sized cardboard box (available free behind your nearest supermarket), painted with joyful mottoes and coated with Scotch tape, will be a shining feature of any closet or playroom. You can keep old Christmas cards in it, too!

RUBBER BAND SNAKES

Cut a rubber band and presto, you've got a toy snake! Give a set of the snake family to nieces and nephews and pray they don't try to swallow them. With things the way they are, a lot of adults are still playing with toys, so give them snakes too!

CHRISTMAS CARD DECORATIONS

I get tired of looking at my old Christmas card collection, since the ones from previous years never change, so I "freshen" them by pasting on interesting phrases and punctuation torn from magazines, or photographs of old schoolmates, or just labels from canned goods. Some of my old cards have been "refreshed" so much I can't remember what they first looked like! Tear out hundreds of interesting phrases, punctuation, and pictures; fireproof them; put them in an old cigar box, and give them to a friend as a labor-saving kit. An old cigar box makes a nice gift in itself. You could even trade boxes of old Christmas cards, and both pretend you have a new set of friends.

There are millions more little objects like these just sitting around my house, and the one I rented next door, plus there was a third one that burned down, but these few notions should help inspire you to sift through your refuse and find the object that's just right for the person you owe a present. And, after all, no law says you can't keep what you find there for yourself!

Xmas Dinner

Imagine it is Christmastime. Across the nation, cocktail waitresses exchange cartons of cigarettes. Divorced mothers give their married teenage children sled-sized boxes of supermarket chocolates. Bulletin boards break out in shredded tinfoil bunting and what appear to be the larva of adult-sized candy canes. Magazines fatten with advertisements, like doomed geese on table scraps, and the smell of holiday baking fills the conversation of the formulaically nostalgic. The world opens its mouth like a caroling choirboy or a coal chute, waiting for the particularly oral tradition of Christmas to sweeten its depths.

The Christmas routine is man's spiritualized rendition of the midwinter hoarded-nuts bash, a practice dating back millions of years, when our species was more of a tree shrew and suckled its young without the benefit of paperback books. The coy greeting-card shorthand for Christmas is *Xmas,* a cavalier revision that by analysis denotes the birthday of Jesus X, presumably an assassinated radical; inasmuch as X symbolizes the unknown quantity, there are sound religious defenses for its use. Besides, some of the most potent icons in Western Christmas culture are X-shaped: the screw-on stand for the Christmas tree; the XXX that comically signifies the labels on liquor bottles; the X through the names of those who failed to give presents last year.

Anyway, you are imagining Christmastime. Using your fine-tuning knob, imagine it is Christmas morning. Snow can be gently falling. That runs you extra. Except for scattered discount drugstores with ambitious branch managers, the workaday world has been put aside. People everywhere rise early (except for a few drug addicts and Jews) to convene on moccasin-tread in the family room for a photogenic session of Gift Exchange. Hallways seem to oscillate in the multiple flash of Polaroid cameras. The air dampens with the smell of raisins, licorice, and perking coffee. Ding Dong Sara Lee on High. And yet, this powwow is mere preliminary to the social-petting-and-grooming that is yet to come, the true participation-through-acquisition that culminates in Christmas dinner.

Dickens and his imitators (of which he is one) have long extolled the figgy splendors of Christmas dinner, and it is their depiction of the "jolly coachman" holiday that doubtless prompts many to drink to violent excess on the occasion. Although boars' heads, flaming puddings, and interesting tablemates are generally limited to the largest of fiction and coffeeshop placemat pictorials, even its theoretical superlativity makes Christmas dinner instructive: It is the Real disappointingly aping the Ideal. Basically, Xmas dinner is Xgiving dinner with a holly centerpiece, but even that is optional. The real difference is that at Christmas, most of the by-now-wilted wassailers have been conceding to pastries and highballs since early in the day, and the meal has no more urgency than a ground-breaking ceremony.

As noon tolls, the house burgeons with grandchildren, busily spilling tumblers of Sprite on carpeted stairways and pounding on the unused piano with a fervor reserved for the musically ignorant. Distant relatives (though clearly, not distant enough) have accumulated in corners with boilermakers and prerehearsed observations on the propensity of others to age and fail. Resident teenagers are brooding upstairs in their rooms, or, if they are gregarious, in the rooms of friends, generally over the pathos of being insufficiently misunderstood. (Acting discontent to be sociable is the first adult skill many youngsters acquire.)

The matriarch of the family, festal queen of the to-do, will be insistently unassisted in the kitchen, doing what sentimentalists call "bustling" and psychoanalysts call "guilt induction." The patriarch, who emerges briefly to carve, is not comfortable in this wave of modern humanity; in company he betrays a noble bewilderment comparable to a Navajo chief set upon by tourists. He generally ends up down in the tool room perusing old Yuban cans full of bolts, or out in the backyard cleaning the rabbit cages.

There is a certain delectation in completeness, and all these types are assembled in much the same spirit as the creamed corn and Brussels sprouts they are about to surround. However, before the gallery sits down to dinner—and I hope you're imagining enough chairs to go around—consider the curiously *visual* function of Christmas food niceties.

Whatever the merits of "Silent Night," Christmas has always been more of an assault on the eyeballs than on any other sensory apparatus. The eye in December learns to regard red and green as a comforting rather than garish combination. Fruitcake, surely, and hard candies in the shape of teensy satin pillows or rigid ruffles, demonstrate the appeal of looking at some foods rather than eating them. The arid, camel-colored cutouts that man recognizes as Christmas cookies and sprinkles with a coruscating confetti of "festive fixin's"—what better illustrates the strange duty of Yule edibles *to be representative art?* Ordinarily, a chocolate chip cookie is just that: a chocolate chip cookie. We don't look at it and say, "Oh, I get it, it's supposed to be the moon, only there are little Nigerian astronauts walking around on it." There is no pressure on it to tell a story. But Christmas cookies must be bells, stars, pine trees, or paddle-limbed humanoids. The mythic abundance of the season crams multiple functions into homely objects, giving them the shape if not the tongue of angels. The quasi-traditional Xmas gingerbread house is the most perverse elaboration on narrative food: a dolly cottage shingled in cookies and heavily marketed by companies who also urge you to give cheese wheels as bon voyage gifts. Here the food lurches into three dimensions, gets even more dry and dusty with not being eaten, and parades about as far from a wholesome life-style for itself as food can get. Its contrivances are meant to titillate the viewer into greater hunger, exploiting a primordial urge to eat one's home. But, while it is "too nice" to eat, no one minds. (Similarly, if people actually *like* candy canes, why are they always around the house, even in midsummer, like currency left over from a foreign vacation? Most families liquidate their candy cane stock by giving it out as Xoween treats. Even a child senses that there must be something wrong with candy canes, otherwise, why would every institution he visits after December first give him one *free?*)

Admittedly, Easter and Halloween treats are also visual, and Mexicans have those wax candy skulls, which could muddle things, but quick, your imaginary relatives have been cooling their heels long enough. Let us free them from the limbo of your mental freeze-frame. A morass of winter's defrosted bounty reclines before them, shinier than trophies and warmer than a hired escort. The board is groaned over admiringly (Christmas dinner being one of those three-ring meals that require a gestalt appraisal), and a conscientiously romantic soul observes it's a shame to eat it. Through the courtesy of all available piano stools and phone books, everyone is sitting, except for the matriarch, who daubs at her work like a model railroader. Exhorted to come to the table, she counters with a self-sacrificial chuckle and retires to the kitchen to load gravy boats. This satisfies her scions, and grace is prefixed to the meal with the briskness of attaching a postage stamp. There follows a Homeric clatter of silverware, and the Extended Family begins extending bowls to each other.

Various prestige guests such as yams or a shivering cylinder of cranberry remind the viewer that this is a holiday. Dull-as-dishwater dishes like peas or celery seem radiant, dressed as they are in the seldom-used good china (a sensation comparable to seeing sitcom stars in high-budget costume dramas). Like a Thanksgiving Day parade, or for that matter, like an armored tank procession through Red Square, the ostentation instructs us to be grateful.

Surprisingly, you and yours manage to put it away pretty extensively. Conversation breaks from the stock-exchange drone in disconnected bursts, and invariably includes the progressive assertion that Ma "really outdid herself this year." After solidarity is thus expressed, the assembly begins to disengage: As coffee arrives, the grandchildren have joined the dog under the table or headed up to the attic to play with Dad's old toys; the teens resume their brooding on a full stomach; the distant relatives resettle like crows after shotgun fire, for further glutinous consultation. Those who left home at an early age help with the dishes. The patriarch stays at table, since it ensures him a little privacy.

In half an hour or so, potato chips and soft drinks are offered and accepted. The stomach, like the heart, persists. Finally, though, heart and stomach are dismissed for the day. Coats, gifts, and children are gathered and counted. Physical exhaustion is interpreted as the glow of intimacy, and relief is read as affection. Involuntarily, the cold tick-tock of accomplishment makes mental check-off marks next to the name of each relation who surfaces within hugging distance. Love can be real without being comfortable.

Imagine the snowfall you imagined earlier has stopped. Car headlights have ceased swooping around the front of the house; the visitors who were visited upon it have gone. A mulch of gift-wrap and ribbons settles underfoot. Leftovers are ignominiously crowded into Tupperware quarters. Forgotten new toys commingle under tables with old toys hauled down from the attic. The day recedes like the tiny dwindling star of a switched-off television screen. Your imaginary house petrifies with silence at that point in the story when the moral is expected, but nothing in the air officializes.

Unplug the tree, putting out the lights as if you were putting out the cat. Eat a cookie for consolation. Christmas and its undelivered epiphany darken, as any object would, under the influence of distance, or falling night, or the exhaustion of the mind obliged to imagine it.

Swimming Taught Scientifically

Dear Friend—Please do not throw this letter away, as you probably have so many others before this. We seek no unfair profit, only what is natural for a valuable service competently offered. We of the School of Swimming Taught Scientifically remind you, especially you shut-ins and pathologically shy types, that we can get you out of your piles of old newspaper and faded religious etchings, and into the turbulent bounding main—without costly traveling expenses, without fear of drowning, *without water.*

Yes, if you have five minutes and an ordinary chair, we can teach you to swim by mail. No instructor will intimidate you, no horizon daunt you. You teach yourself with any one of our ten scientific pamphlets and fold-out lifelike watery-blue floor patterns. Choose from the backstroke, the trudgen crawl, treading water, the catherine wheel, swimming like a dog, swimming like a cat that didn't want to be thrown in, swimming with clothes on, swimming with hands and feet tied, the Monte Cristo sack trick, and the successful English Channel crossing. As a bonus if you order all ten, we will include a free instruction manual on artificial artificial respiration.

You probably imagine yourself to be open-minded. How can you presume to judge us without trying our methods? Why throw this letter away when you could be open-minded and send us a check or money order? Do you suppose we have enjoyed the meager response to our previous mailings? Why should you live your life in fear, either of us or of the oceans that cover most of our earth? Complete the enclosed blank and return it with your offering.

Don't delay. Summer is short and so is life.

Strangers in Town

Hank was an only child, and his parents let him know he was their destiny. They were conservative people, but they liked expansion, so figured it would be best to concentrate their investment in one child. They were Texans, self-made Houstonites who trusted no one, so had to be friendly to everyone, a policy they handed on to Hank by christening him with a nickname. Thanks to vitamins, he grew up tall, which people interpreted as rectitude, and he was oblivious enough to converse effortlessly, which people interpreted as intelligence. His self-confidence sprang from an only child's disbelief in the reality of others, though their belief in him convinced him of his own, so he was habitually ingratiating. When he graduated first in his business school class, his friends gave him a farewell joke trophy, a welded concoction bristling with chrome figures of a bowler, golfer, female swimmer, airplane, and even a dog. The tribute was humorous because his friends thought that would better conceal their jealousy. The farewell was because Hank liked expansion too, so had accepted a job in a New York advertising agency and was in his view ascending there to a broader challenge, to see if people not obliged to be friendly would approve him. It was in New York that he met Priss, Margaret, Pony, and Mutt.

Priss weighed less than her twin brother at birth, and remained in second place as they grew up, since her sober Bostonian parents were old-fashioned and favored boys. She wasn't prissy, but was too shy as a child to forbid the nickname's taking hold. In fact, she was pretty and smart, but doubted both, so people got the impression she was neither. Puberty made her quarrel with her twin and he proceeded to Dartmouth ("Voice Crying in the Desert"), she to Radcliffe ("Truth"). He became a soccer star there, while she wallowed insecurely in the Economics major her parents advised for her security. Her only glory was as Mary Queen of Scots in a house dramatic production: she obediently followed her director's instructions to be commanding, and was. Her only sex life was with a black Kenyan graduate student, an adventure rather than an investment, since she knew from fiction that one doesn't marry the first one. When her parents met him at graduation, she didn't tell them he'd been her boyfriend, and they chose not to assume it. They concentrated instead on loading her things in a rented truck to move her to New York. Her father had arranged a job interview for her at an advertising agency, and, crucial to her decision, her best friend Margaret was joining her in what Margaret called their "kamikaze life pact."

Margaret loved Priss's cleansing blondness and self-effacing plainness, and Priss loved Margaret's spirited blue-collar banter and liberated plainness. Margaret was from Cleveland, not Shaker Heights but depressed, Slavic, broken-down Cleveland itself, so she was guilty of pride. Her family's poverty served her well, because she got a scholarship to Radcliffe, where her love of gossip and the outlandish prompted her to major in Psychology. Her parents were amicably divorced, so she'd been reared to thrive on thorny wisecracks, an inheritance her co-workers feared and enjoyed. She was so sarcastic people could guess she was a virgin. When she decided to move to New York after graduation to study language acquisition in apes with a Columbia professor, her friends at the lab gave her a fully assembled Visible Woman and a signed mash note from King Kong. She was also the cause of wit in others, which was what Mutt would love in her.

Mutt pretended to be stupid for the sake of his Italian father, and shiftless so his Irish mother could fulfill herself by waiting on him. He was a healthy ten-pounder, christened Matthew and reared in South Boston, where it was to his social advantage to slouch and feign worthlessness. He was a sensation as Frank Sinatra one Halloween, and as a result let traces of the impersonation govern him thereafter. He bypassed college as a gesture of solidarity with his overage hoodlum brothers. Actually, he was a good carpenter and discovered women would sleep with him if he built them bookcases or tables. Eventually, their recommendations led to his doing woodwork for strangers. He'd done some repair work for Priss's father and was recommended by him to fix up Priss and Margaret's New York apartment. He had a van and friends in an NYU fraternity he could stay with, so he took the job. That's when he met Margaret and Priss, and Hank and Pony.

Pony (a nickname he coined and desperately promoted himself) was born in Salt Lake City, premature and underweight, disadvantages he exploited to get his way over his three elder sisters and mother. His father, in observance of the Mormon motto of Industry, had died of a heart attack (he was a secret coffee drinker) when Pony was two years old. As a result, his sisters and mother spoiled him, which made him underestimate feminine approval and long for masculine affirmation. He grew up nice-looking in a commercial Mormon way, but his height (five foot four) reduced him to cute. Like many children who are overindulged and sense it, he was self-involved and self-doubtful simultaneously, which— coupled with a scrupulous lack of briefing on the facts of life— ultimately expressed itself as homosexuality. He was not smart, which went undetected in his set, but he was limber and could play the guitar, which led him to sing morale-boosters for his church youth gatherings, as compensation for his secret evil and as a means to exhibit himself. Since college can be considered superfluous for guitar players, he chose to take a bus to New York and be discovered. It was ill-considered but that didn't mean it had to be ill-fated.

. . .

Once at Ringer and Bellman (the ad agency), Hank was quickly distinguished as a leader, since he made inconsequential decisions without hesitation. Even the personnel director asked Hank whom he liked among job applicants. When Priss was interviewed, Hank liked her in the corridor and gave his boss the go-ahead. Priss had canceled her first interview because she became ill over it, and concentrated on watching Mutt fix up the new apartment, though Margaret warned her, "Food before nest." The second scheduled interview went smoothly, since her father had been promised she would get the job, and her interviewer had decided to be friendly to her to entertain himself. The only flub that haunted her was her improvised confession that she'd wished she'd majored in Psychology, for advertising's sake, and didn't know why she hadn't majored in Psychology, but if she had perhaps she could explain why she hadn't. She got the job.

Margaret had sustained Priss through her counterfeit illness with jokes about resenting her helplessness, and also managed Mutt, who, finding his employers helpless, had great fun by teasing them and behaving like a friendly gorilla: it took him a month to do a two-week job. Sleeping in a partly painted apartment by shifting from room to room depressed Priss, whose people were not nomadic, so Margaret had to rally for them both, especially to check Mutt's unwitting sexual displays. It was the longest audition Mutt had ever had.

Pony and his secretly acquired mirrored sunglasses arrived at Port Authority at twilight. He stepped from his bus into the chaser lights, maniac evangelists, erotica stands, and prerecorded church bells of Times Square. A prostitute he politely refused taunted him for being gay, which he took as a sign that city dwellers see through everything remorselessly. Unnerved, he stuck to his YMCA room, secretly suspecting there might be a cheaper place to stay, eating cookies he kept in the provided dresser, and writing clumsy guitar ballads about being cooped up in a room. His endless practicing was poignant, but his songs were not. Finally he felt shrewd by buying and scanning the listed casting calls in the trade papers. He needed actor's photos, but cut up his posed family picture for the first tryout he resolved to brave.

Told he was ineligible for the television commercial role he applied for, he took his undersize trapezoidal photo and handwritten credits to the agency involved, assuming they would think of him next time. As it happened, Hank saw Pony trying to convince Priss, who was filling in for the receptionist, to keep the picture, though she protested that they did no casting there. Pony demonstrated his Elvis—you could tell it was Elvis because the song was "Blue Suede Shoes"—though softly, since he knew enough not to make a scene. Hank was entertained, since Texans love odd anecdotes, and felt beholden to Pony after retelling the scene several times, so got him called for a caffeine-free cola commercial requiring nonthreatening rambunction. Pony got the job.

Priss began her job before Margaret's summer vacation ended (her professor summered in the jungle), so Margaret found herself alone with Mutt. He had established a courtship with both girls as a safe joke, but circumstances found him inviting Margaret to visit him at adoptive fraternity sometime. She was lonely—Priss had met Hank and was busy conjecturing—and unconsciously frightened by her building's creepy superintendent, whose vague sexual bids had turned to sullen unavailability when they were overlooked. Half interested and half frightened of future plumbing problems, she visited Mutt, at his specifically vague suggestion, unexpectedly, the following night. She found him flipping rude jokes about a porno video he and some sophomores were screening. She had respected his lowness but this she felt called for anger on principle, since no graceful date could follow anyway. Luckily, he had only one more day's work on the Casa Kamikaze, as Margaret called it. They parted badly, which planted the sensation of a romance in them.

Hank took Priss on an Upper West Side date: cartoons at the

Thalia, where an audience of adults laughed at a Thirties Looney
Tune of premarital violence between two pigs. Despite this potential damper, they managed to align via Chinese food, and had sex
at Hank's apartment. Since both were new in New York they assumed it was the polite standard. They got along so well Hank
decided it was better she not spend the night. They parted
vaguely, which, coupled with the August humidity, planted the
sensation of a romance in them.

Pony, and a group of bikini-clad adults who played adolescents
professionally, filmed the commercial, circling the Statue of Liberty on a tugboat spruced up for the occasion, dancing with well-
rehearsed abandon and waving bottles of Yes at the westward horizon. After hours, the wholesome-looking cast introduced Pony to
cocaine, pot, and overly social drinking. He had been carefully
reared, so had no ready resistance. He became known as Mister
Twist and Shout, but only after a certain point in the evening.
Hank appeared at the shooting several times, always in the morning, so Pony associated him with paternal strength and hard work.
Hank was automatically encouraging to Pony, which planted the
sensation of a romance in Pony.

Mutt and Margaret had a difficult phone call, since he was
helpless when his Frank Sinatra act was inappropriate. Her insults, however, convinced him she believed in his better self. Pow-
ered by inanition, he remained in town and got a job as a bicycle
messenger. Since his co-workers were all uneducated black teenagers, he took this as a sign of his savvy and validity. Margaret was
attracted to Mutt—he was big, dumb, and sexy, like the universe—but feared his good temper and interest in her proved he
had no ambition. Then, in the tradition of expanding frustration,
her impending employer was accused of falsifying data. Much had
been made of his spectacular report that a chimp he had trained
to speak sign language had, in a moment of anger, spontaneously
combined the symbols for excrement and rotten food with the sign
for the professor's name. A colleague claimed this was a fiction for

publicity, and demanded duplication of results. The controversy suspended Margaret's beginning work, and the sensation of joblessness in New York opened beneath her.

Priss assumed Hank could never love her, and subtly encouraged him to vindicate her belief. Actually, he assumed he loved Priss, since he felt aimlessly comfortable with her apparent self-sufficiency. Before he could tell her, though, he was sent on a publicity tour as the sudden co-author of a book. His boss had moonlighted a hopeful self-help best-seller called *You Can Make Them Like You*, but was so grating and ugly his publishers felt a front man was needed for top talk-show impact. Hank was so appealing his boss returned to work and let him complete the tour himself, and the book did very well, further proof to Priss that Hank's life was too full to add her. She was lonely because she lacked even herself.

Pony projected his movie fantasies of rescue on the screen of Hank's white shirts, and dogged him with the imperviousness of the gauche among the gracious. His swizzle of a Yes was used to cap the commercial, and he got more ad work; his inner confusion gave him an expression directors felt an audience could relate to. He next played an older brother bested by his toddler competitor's fleet of toy trucks, and then the person least likely to understand computers finally understanding one. He joined a guild and got an agent, in exchange for which God-sent bribe he reflexively volunteered celibacy, another of the secret scandals of show business. However, his deal with God allowed him drugs and alcohol.

Priss and Margaret's spurned super implied he knew it was they who had spray-painted obscenities on their elevator walls, since Priss and Margaret were the youngest residents, and he didn't know about Radcliffe. This eerie fillip roused them to organize a Labor Day weekend escape. They rented a car, just like Manhattan adults, who unlike their parents have casual relations with many cars rather than buy one and take care of parking. Priss invited Hank, whose compulsive courtesy forced him to invite

Pony, who was standing in Hank's office when Priss phoned. Pony was to balance the picture, and hence Margaret's pride, Hank later realized he had reasoned.

The weekend was a rout of skew interests; without surrounding noise, New York dementia enters bold relief. On the drive up, Pony tried to break the rented-car ice by leading the singing of rounds, unaware it maddened his companions. "All things shall perish from under the sky, Music alone shall live, never to die" was his last gambit as they sighted Priss's family's Cape Cod beach house. Mutt, wet from a swim, was waiting on the porch when they arrived. He had come uninvited and unwelcome as a heroic gesture, and Margaret lambasted him, though with a rubber-tipped pitchfork, since she was secretly riveted by his rudeness for love's sake. Pony was disappointed by the existence of Priss, but was guiltily sunny to her. His attentions to her made Priss sense he was her rival, though she was impressed with the grown-up feeling of it. Margaret had decided not to like Hank, as a safety balance for infatuated Priss's sake, and was stymied by his charm when she finally spent time with him. Mutt's ironic boorishness confused literal-minded Pony, and Pony's loud-mouthed inhibitedness made the group inwardly reckon him a tormented deputy of the Born Again, even though he'd barely been born once. Hank vaguely sensed the disparities, but believed it was kindest not to acknowledge trouble until necessary, so felt that entitled him not to consider it.

Pony, gladdened by wine, sang around the fire, which made Priss and Hank begin to glaze, and Mutt led Margaret out for a walk when Pony took a break to deliver patter between songs.

On the moonlit beach, Margaret remembered a chaos even more basic than Cleveland. She commented on the scuttling and striving of the crabs and beached fish, and that the tides of the ocean and of animal appetite expressed the inexorable pulsation and impinging gravities of the subparticles of the Big Bang. Mutt tenderly agreed, and they made love. He was surprised by her virginity, and that flattered her. It was awkward, but she didn't know enough to resent the gritty sand, and he found it an exotic change from the convenient. Afterward, she wondered aloud if there were a word for happy and sad at once. Mutt suggested sappy.

Hank and Priss also excused themselves from Pony and retired to make love, but secreted in and surrounded by civilization, in the form of a room with a secure door. Believing he didn't love her made Priss cherish their sex. Wishing to be helpful, Hank said he loved her. After he fell asleep, Priss wondered what was taking the inevitable crisis.

Mutt and Margaret returned to find Pony passed out on the porch, having consoled himself into stupefaction. They put him to bed and proceeded to theirs warm with their own charity. Just at dawn, sleepless Priss took a walk on the beach, tense with the chilly air and waves, but borne up by their authoritative recommendation of acceptance. She had just decided to accept when she saw a young couple on an unsaddled horse ride by through the surf's edge, man and woman naked to the waist, their bare legs knit like twins in a womb. Priss winced at its preposterously standard beauty. Back at the house she put on coffee, and when Margaret emerged, announced to her she was going to get psychiatric help. Margaret, having majored in Psychology, discouraged her, but primarily to downplay Priss's problems and proceed to outline her own new hopes and imaginings. Sexual knowledge had shattered Margaret's worldliness.

Back in the city, Pony decided to spurn Hank as punishment for being unaware of him. Happily for him, Pony was next cast in a movie, *The Stranger from Earth,* a low-budget fantasy in which he starred as the lovable laird of a desert-island-sized asteroid, ultimately master to a blue-skinned beauty and, after the film, the figurehead of a massive merchandising argosy. He went to Hollywood and gave up drinking, and in exchange at last he could have all the sex he wanted. He didn't feel people saw through him out there.

Hank shivered when Pony retracted his approval, since it was an unfamiliar feeling, and again later when Pony's hit movie made the loss seem more substantial. Priss receded from Hank as well, at first to test his interest but finally to keep her restored breathing regular. Hank might have tried to keep her, but he felt bullied when he interpreted her request for a separation as a request for marriage, so had to resist it by surrendering to it. Eventually, he left the agency and became a talk-show host, a beloved short-term listener, applauded on videotapes he could save. His guests on *Success Talk* were famous unmarried couples and concocted teen stars who recited with conceited frankness how they managed careers and real identities. To their undemanding narcissism Hank turned the one-way mirror of his eyes and reassured them they existed. At last he overcame his many advantages, and found a verifiable reality.

Priss went to a psychiatrist several times, but his insidious silence so reminded her of her superintendent she asked not to continue with him. He forbade it, since she had so far to go, but for once she declined sponsorship and left his office. He yelled after her that she would never be free. However, as she discovered the competence born of indifference, she was promoted at Ringer and Bellman and was often asked out. Her Kenyan ex-boyfriend, now engaged, passed through New York and they slept together, expecting nothing from it. It was the best sex she'd ever had. At last she found her way out of the dark forest of hope.

Mutt's messenger service decided to upgrade its image and fired all its employees but Mutt, which was a blow to his self-respect. His bosses' plan was to recast themselves as Preppin' Fetchit, and provide a white adult in Brooks Brothers clothes to run any client's errands. It was a great success, but without Mutt, who regarded neckties as unmasculine. Luckily, the next trapeze arrived before he could tumble: in the tradition of expanding good fortune, he lucked into a loft that was unreasonably rather than impossibly overpriced, and there built furniture on commission for his neighbors' friends. Margaret moved in with him. At last he transcended his fraternal urge to underreach himself.

Margaret's job came through when her boss was cleared, at least inasmuch as his accuser was discovered to have fabricated many of the most horrifying anecdotes in his famous book on the effects of overcrowding on rats. Margaret was a hit with staff and apes alike, and Mutt often joined her at the lab to watch admiringly as she trained a young chimp to sign. They would have made a lovely scene, if anyone had seen them: the virtual virgin, her carpenter husband, their miraculous child. At last Margaret could believe in modern family life.

Dear John

June 25

Dear John,
~~The funniest thing abo~~
~~Life is so odd when y~~
~~Just think. You introduced me to Wa~~
Call my mother and ask her how I am.

Love,
~~Mrs. Walte~~
Joan

Cupidity and Psyche

The dominant trend in business today is toward *enlightened ruthlessness*. Just as one can Meditate to Better Racquetball, so can modern execs Zen Their Way to Power by advertising a less-competitive-than-thou superiority. Some adherents complain that to win by not wanting to win, however, requires them actually *not* to want to—a bind comparable to the fairytale dilemma of the flying carpet that will fly only if the owner really doesn't care if it does or not. Others prefer retreading Christian thought, and learn to Pray More Dynamically, or arrange to be born again very noisily, to show their solidity and the conquering depth of their resolves.

Most of all, though, *psychology* has reared its convoluted head in business practice. The corridors of Everyman's mind, once the strict province of sideshow memory prodigies, are now open to observation and strip-mining by any with patience and a magazine article telling them what to see. By becoming a "people" person, an executive no longer causes thoughtless damage to those around him. His new sensitivity enables him to calculate and direct the damage with unprecedented accuracy. Moreover, his (or her, since women have joined the demo derby) own thoughts, like the ox entrails of Attic augurers, can be appraised for meaning. The twittering chaff of the mind, yours or your opponent's, can be spun into gold with the following modicum of study.

EXPLOITING OTHERS: APPLIED FREUD

Children instinctively know how to hurt each other's feelings, but some adults allow this precious faculty to atrophy. The study of the subconscious is of great help to those whose natural viciousness is in remission, but Freud à la Machiavelli requires extensive physical props.

If the chairs in your reception area have undersized oval seats, your adversaries (and putative comrades) will enter your office unwittingly shaken and humbled by the subtle reminder of potty training they have just so dimly endured. A maternal-looking receptionist who praises others in the waiting room (whom you have expressly hired for this purpose), but ignores Your Chosen Target, will promote his sense of unworthiness. A softly lit, womb-shaped reception area is not a bad idea either; when clients are ejected from it into your presence, the ritualized birth trauma leaves them limp and acquiescent.

Your own Den of Inequity should be maximized for subliminal aggression. Camouflaged furniture (i.e., upholstered to match the carpet) will be much tripped over, delicately reminding visitors they are on your turf, and less in control than you. Few people will be impressed by Dark Daddy symbols such as desktop pipes or clipper ship paperweights, since most of them cravenly strew their own cubicles with the same flotsam of the Masculine Mystique. However, there is still fresh intimidation to be had from savage tabletop plants, heavy polished spheres circling the floor on electrified tracks, and discreet piles of moist cattle bones. Also, by making the doorway to your office only two feet high, you can insure that the caller will enter not only with hat in hand, but on hands and knees. Receiving, or better yet, making phone calls during your transaction will trumpet your might as only rudeness can, and incidentally reinforce your mark's inborn suspicion that he isn't interesting enough.

When it comes to humbling your competitor, though, it helps no end to customize your skulduggery to whatever you can learn about his or her infant years and prevailing neuroses. For instance, suppose an unwanted baby survives abandonment in a trash can and grows up to eminence as a maritime lawyer, albeit your rival. Imagine his uneasiness when you seat him in such a receptacle during negotiations, while you blandly observe how challenging high-tech furniture styles can be. "Static on the intercom" can be your excuse for piped-in rat gabbling, and a long-suppressed sense of loneliness will well up and unman him, enabling you to write your own ticket to the high seas.

Or suppose your files show that a troublesome client was a bedwetter at summer camp, decades ago. Show him to a seat and yawn visibly. He will reflexively imitate you, at which point you ask if he enjoyed his nap. Bewildered, he will protest that he does not recall falling asleep. You give a wan smile and proceed with business. After a few seconds, the client will sense a dampness in his chair seat (since the cushion on it is a laden sponge specially placed there) and will begin his inevitable collapse. You evince nothing but indulgent indifference, possibly referring to him as a "homesick little fella" as you outline your proposals, or venturing an enigmatic glance at his trousers. Before long he will be as malleable as the once-and-future toddler many were born to be.

From here, the possibilities are obvious: rubber tarantulas, coffee meetings on sickeningly high ledges, bathroom doors with a disconcerting tendency to lock from the outside—the tactics are as myriad as the varieties of submerged human discomfort. Admittedly, there are a few benign ways to appeal to others' attachments to past emotional events; there have been instances of go-getters dressing up as their customer's favorite childhood gollywog or plush toy, to lucrative results. However, shame is a more volatile commodity than nostalgia, and has built more empires. Even Freud said that.

EXPLOITING YOURSELF: ANALYZE YOUR DREAMS

Ever since Joseph used his dreams about cows to forecast Egyptian business prospects for the Pharaoh, opportunistic men have tried to wring from their sleeping fantasies benefits for their waking hours. Dreams may not foretell the future, but they do illuminate the present, which, finally, is simply the menu for whatever the Fates have on ice for you elsewhere, be it champagne or crow.

Many businessmen will say, "But I don't dream," and many more will say, "But I can't sleep," and if you are either or both of these men, dream analysis is as hypothetical for you as unicorn vivisection. However, if you do sleep, and perchance dream as well, you have a lucrative source of input about your current situation as close as your own head. If you can pay attention while unconscious, you can learn a lot about yourself, and at considerably less expense than hiring a biographer.

Consider this example:

I am at home with my wife when slowly I realize the furniture is sinking into the floor, as if it were quicksand. Lamps, wine racks, and our new video center all disappear beneath the deep-pile carpet. I call to my wife, but she seems not to hear. I tell her to get the children out, but she is already slipping down into the carpet herself. Somehow I escape.

This dream's lush sense of self-protective hysteria advises its owner (you, let's say) to become a market analyst. If the worst happens, your foresight will be admired. If good things happen instead, the peace of plenty will forgive your zeal to sight danger. In any case it reminds you to escape.

Or relive this classic pillow-twister:

I stop at the newsstand before a big conference and the old guy who sells me a pack of Certs points out that I'm not wear-

ing any clothes. Covering myself with my attaché case as best I can, I take the elevator up to the penthouse offices where the conference is to be. Murmurs greet my arrival, and I debate whether to make an excuse or ignore it. Instead, I burst into tears. My boss says, "If only you hadn't cried," and my promotion falls away into darkness.

The dangers of self-revelation are well-known, and particularly in business it is inadvisable to be understood. This dreamer's failure is not so much nudity (we are all nude underneath) as it is vulnerability. The Certs, after all, "cover up" bad breath, as our clothes cover us. Luckily, any adulterer (you, come on) knows that although nakedness seems to stand for self-exposure, one's real secrets remain protected. Our dreamer should endlessly worry what others think of him, of course, but with yeomanly reason he can curb his tears and brazen out any display of rump required.

Many report having this next dream, but few have seen it in its uncut form:

I somehow miss my stop on the commuter train and continue into the wilds. Animals standing on their hind legs and foreign-looking people dressed as animals begin to fill the car, which suddenly springs with tendrilous tropical vegetation. It gets as black as night outside, and a great wind starts to shake the car. I feel a pitch and roll under my feet, and realize the train is floating in space, writhing, serpentine, as it were, in a void. The animals and foreigners grin to reveal sharpened teeth. I pass out, which means I wake up, as they circle 'round me.

Curiously, this dream is reported more often by Republicans than Democrats, though the latter group usually describe an interval in which they offer the foreigners and animals money. In either case, such a dream bespeaks a xenophobia that would well suit a personnel director at a bank. Its conservatism suggests caution in foreign investments and a healthy distrust of excess; in this case, "going too far" on one's train.

Here is another, less fraught dream whose bottom line may at first seem unfathomable:

> *I am not even in this dream. There is a large rock, several large rocks, in fact, sitting in a row. They're boulders, if you want to know the truth. The weather is overcast, and the rocks just sit there and sit there. Hours go by. The rocks are still there. I smell coffee perking somewhere.*

Whoever has a dream like this is the stuff of which great executive vice-presidents are made. Dependability, scrupulous attention to detail, and satisfaction with orderly appearances will rocket their holder to a well-upholstered subordinate position. There is a further popular appeal to this personality, insofar as it generously dreams about subjects other than itself. While this may hinder it from absolute power, such self-effacement will be routinely advanced a great distance, the way innocuous-looking luggage breezes through customs.

Strangely, few would-be or even are-dammit-are successes ever report dreaming about money itself—in piles, bags, or even the fabled swimming pool full of it. Since money most directly denotes power, since it is the bricks that build man's ego igloo, why does it figure so slightly in dreamscapes? Consider this exceptional chimera, visited upon the fitful sleep of a New York broker:

> *Somehow I'm living on the Isle of Yap, where all the money is made of stone and cut into coins seven feet in diameter. I think my son was reading to me from Ripley's before I went to bed. Anyway, I have to open an account at the local bank,*

since I'm new on Yap, and I take my assets to American Express to be converted. They tell me that each of these seven-foot stone wheels are worth about seventy cents American and start to pile them on my outstretched arms. I played intramural football at school, but I can't carry a hundred thousand dollars in millstones. My arms start to ache and the pile of coins stretches up into the sky. It really hurts and my wife says to me, "Are you sure you can handle that, Keith? Shall I call your brother?" Every time I have this dream I wake up in a sweat with my legs aching. Once I was standing on the bathroom scale holding our extra bedding.

Actually, who knows what it means? Avoid cultures that haven't discovered credit?

Soon to Be a Major Motion Picture

Jana, a beautiful, independent young designer of men's fashion underwear, is asked by her dowdy male boss to work late when their upcoming fall preview requires it. She rebels, accompanied by a chart-busting musical theme, although her timid co-workers agree to stay late for double time and a half.

Frustrated by the system, which also forbids her to design men's fashion underwear for women, Jana takes matters into her own hands. After donating her designs for men's fashion underwear for women to a local day-care center, she takes her down jacket and a rifle to the skyscraper roof opposite her firm's penthouse offices, and threatens to shoot her boss, who is having a desk-top extramarital affair when Jana's warning shot shatters his office picture window.

Raf, a handsome young TV newsman, not the usual phony, but crusading and funky, but handsome, don't forget, arrives on the rooftop to talk her down. They meet cute as she fires around him, shooting leaks in a water tank that drench his suit. His hair remains dry, ready for a masculine-hold hairspray tie-in.

At this point Jana's co-workers, male and female, black and white, see the wisdom of her approach and to stop her threaten to shoot her. A psychologist dispatched to the scene to talk them out of it becomes afraid to take sides and jumps to his death. Jana, frightened by this violence, turns to Raf for comfort. While his live minicam picks up her every tearful reflection on what has brought

her to this, she builds an involuntary intimacy with her interviewer.

Jana's boss is desperate, however. His fall fashion preview is
about to begin in the ballroom on the first floor of the building,
and he fears that a potential assassin will discourage attendance.
He makes a deal with Jana via megaphone: He'll pay her not to
work late, and he'll reveal his extramarital affair to his wife via
Raf's live TV camera. Raf thinks it's very honest. Jana also de-
mands that her boss remove his toupee and do a little dance on
the ledge. He does. Now, it seems, everything will be fine. Jana
lowers her rifle.

Suddenly, a shot rings out, and Jana disappears from sight.
On the office side, her boss's dowdy wife (who's arrived unexpectedly after seeing her husband on television) has fired a pistol at
Jana and is leaning out to see if she aimed true. The boss's now
fully dressed steno-mistress runs to the wife's side. Jana's face appears from behind a chimney opposite: She's all right!

There is a struggle for the gun on the office side, since the
boss's mistress wants to fire the second shot at Jana, and in the
mutual eagerness, the probably-henna-haired mistress falls out
the broken window to her requisite end.

Horrified, Jana buries her head in Raf's shoulder. Across the
street, the boss and his wife reconcile. Soft hit music. Jana and
her co-workers hurl their firearms away, to rain harmlessly on pas-
sersby below, and she and they take opposite elevators down to the
street level. Arm in arm with Raf, she follows her boss and his
wife into the fall fashion preview. She's not dressed for it but she
carries it off. Top-forty triumphal recessional.

Consumer Therapy

Dear C. T.—

I have never been the center of attention in anyone's life, and since I am over fifty I must accept that I may be alone for the rest of my days. This, however, is complicated by an inexplicable hatred which my nephew, a recent college dropout, apparently feels for me. In the three months since he moved to my town, he has telephoned many friends of mine—and my employer—to warn them about what he calls my "hypocrisy" and my "will to hurt." He never encouraged my company, but I always sent little gifts for appropriate holidays. I can't imagine why he would upset the only human contact I have. He was once arrested for forgery but that was years ago.

SHATTERED IN RAVENSBURG

What's the purchase to perk up a scenario like this? Linen and household goods—The white sales are now on, and a vast new bath towel to wrap around yourself could be a buffering comfort. A plump bedrest for bedtime reading will serve you on those sleepless nights. Little ceramic figurines might help.

Dear C. T.—

I admit that my carelessness at a summer job in a hotel kitchen allowed a friend of mine to die (this was in high school), but much has happened in the years since then, and I have tried to act with new moral and spiritual purpose. Still, the vision of my negligence has surfaced in my dreams recently, and I can't sleep. My wife says I'm so jumpy I seem to be expecting a crucial phone call. I can't concentrate on my work. Barry's drowned face looms before me, and I don't know what I should do to atone or resolve. His family forgave me, though none of them can bear to speak to me without wincing. There's nothing I can act upon.

OBSESSED IN HARMONY FALLS

You can redo your den. Imagine how the workers' ongoing confusion in there will distract you. A new room modifies the basic rules of living with yourself, the way a haircut entitles you to feel more concise. And a new kitchen sink might rekindle your belief in cleanliness before death.

Dear C. T.—

If I'd known that old age was as heartbreaking as this, I would have lived in terror of it since my childhood. As it is, my children have deserted me, an ironic slap since all eight of them were adopted. (My late husband was a sensitive man who greatly feared communicable diseases.) Although we saved them from poverty they live on their trust funds in distant cities, leaving me with only strangers and service people to tell about my illness and inexperience. It's like being under a witch's spell, and no one in the world knows who I am. It's hard to want to go on.

DESPERATE IN EDGEWATER

Many silk or paper flowers have a beauty that isn't plasticky at all. Stylized and unnaturalistic ones are often the prettiest, and they require no care once they're placed somewhere. Real plants are nice to tend, but artificial ones are even better if you're not sure anyone will be around to take care of them.

Dear C. T.—

The torment is unreal. I have been in love with my twin brother's wife for twenty years. We had one night of solace, but since
then Gemma and I have respected Dan's rights. What is strange,
though, is that their only child was born about nine months after
our indiscretion. The boy looks like me, of course, but he looks
like Dan just as much. The youngster is bright, virile, popular, and
destined for a virtuous greatness that makes the people in this
town weep with awe. Is he my son? I have no other children. I
must know, but not even Gemma knows.

DAMNED IN CLIFFVIEW

*Chances are your car can do with a few more essential luxuries.
A leather steering wheel cover makes driving more of an experience, and a good tape system is easily installed. You can turn the
volume way up as you drive and be able to hear nothing else.*

Le Dernier Cri

What a week! Is everyone on earth as sick of crabmeat mousse as I am? All the clubs must be using the same caterer, because for the last five track-lit nights I've been losing my mind eating the same thing. I'm going to stop going to press receptions unless it's to publicize a very close friend. I mean it.

Fortunately, Devienne Blair is a close friend, so I forgive her old-hat banquet at Fata Morgana last Monday. Big Devi's been in New Wave-a York exactly three years now, and her videos about herself keep getting better and better. What's not getting better is Fata's projection screen. If you advertise a giant five-story video screen the resolution should be better—I barely recognized Devi except for her trademark eyepatch-worn-where-the-third-eye-would-be. No wonder the videotti call the place Fatal Moronic under their breath while they eat the crabmeat mousse. Devi tried to kill owner Vito Gee, and I don't blame her.

Leetha La Mount's non-birthday party was the same night at the Club Mondo. I suppose it was wonderful, everyone weeping and undressing and crying with ecstasy and hugging and accepting expensive presents from Tiffany's, and of course those circus people joined Leetha onstage around three a.m. to sing a song celebrating her Eppie award for best skin. They acted like old friends but I doubt they even have any friends in common. (My probably brilliant conceptual actor friend Grey Gordian says that any given person is just one or two steps from royalty, if you connect everyone they've slept with with everyone *they've* slept with. If you care.) Anyway, I know how moved everyone was, rolling on the waxed floor and hoping Leetha would never die, but the whole thing just left me cold somehow. I shouldn't have tried to do both bashes, I guess. I was tired, and Roy Raushenbaum's daughter Royelle kept following me around being arch in her Hefty-bag gown, hoping to get in my column. Now leave me alone, Royelle, go make those dull videos about yourself for the Pizzadrome. She has some growing up to do. Anyway, everyone else enjoyed it, Devi even showed up after the fire at Fata Morgana, so I'm not passing judgment. But it did bore me, just to be factual. Of course I did pass out, too, I'd been at receptions since noon. (The Museum of Intentionally Bad Art had a funny afternoon thing but it was too early for normal people to be out and there were so many nine-to-fivers playing hooky I nearly suffocated. A couple of people came up and asked me if, the way I was dressed, I was part of the exhibit. It doesn't pay to go slumming innovatively garbed. I only liked one thing out of the whole huge exhibit, and that was Sex Butterworth's *Color Xerox of a Photo of a Drawing of Michelangelo's David.* It obviates everything Michelangelo ever did, with its witty multidimensionality. He didn't know who'd done the drawing, though. Sex is a good friend of Grey's, but neither of them will tell me his real name. Butterworth sounds like a male cheerleader at Iowa State, assuming there is an Iowa State. I assume there is.)

But I'm going backwards in time. It must be the levels of my brain being complex. Tuesday night we skipped the Diapers Only party at Jesus Christ's. The whole sacrilege aspect is drawing the dull people, tunnel-taking suburban types who dress as nuns and do poppers in the deconsecrated bell tower. Besides, Grey wanted to go to Royelle Raushenbaum's I'm-an-artist-like-my-Dad affair at Loco. She's so intent on getting in my column, I have to indulge her, even though her hundreds-of-computerized-lights gown wasn't as funny as the dailies said it was. I suggested she swim in the punch to test the wiring insulation, but the dailies didn't even report my quip. So, another scoop for me! Grey was his gracious self, kissing Royelle's breasts all evening long just to help her get in the papers. Royelle's dad did the invitation: Five-foot-tall chunks of cardboard delivered by messengers dressed as messengers, only the invitations were blank. You either knew or you didn't. The chicken Française was okay, though the hired singer (who *was* she?) shouldn't have called Carlo Mangi a bastard just for pulling her shoes off. Instead of filming it all they had a man cutting out little silhouettes of everyone from black paper. In keeping with the Art theme, supposedly, but I lost mine and someone stepped on Grey's. Urge to kill, huh, Grey?

After that happened Grey started getting restless, and Royelle said her breasts had begun to ache, so he started kissing his own arm, *so* then I suggested we use my two comps for the Save-the-Locusts fundraiser at Here Today. We both hate locusts but figured we'd give it a once-over for giggles, and for me, the Raushenbaum clan was starting to pall. I guess I grew beyond them in the course of that evening. Maybe everyone should.

Here Today looks the same since super-rich nonbather (no one complains) Grotto Berliner took over, but in fact he had the whole place torn down and rebuilt upside down, and he and his blond flunkies issue everyone suction boots and rocket belts at the door. My mind was altered as it was, but it still strikes me as eerie as I type this: everything seeming perfectly normal till a waiter would trip, and he and the drinks would go smashing to the ceiling. Pluteau St. Grisby (whose see-through designs were the only things included in the 50,000 A.D. time capsule buried under Drinkateria last week) sat with us and showed off his new variable haircut he'd had done in London. Once you get used to the headache, he says, it's great to be crew cut one minute and Prince Valiant the next. He went to the washroom four times to change styles for us, which took determination since it's hard to walk in suction boots. Finally he let his hair out to mermaid length and we all laughed because of course it seemed to be hanging straight up in the air. Grey kissed him for a while to keep things calm and I noticed that everyone in the place was one of the freebie crowd, so I guess they didn't raise anything to save the locusts. I told Grotto how I hate locusts and he said it was a Save-the-Lotus fundraiser for some Oriental group. Then he showed a video about himself nobody would have paid to see anyway, but they mention me in it so I should try to be nice about it. Everyone got to take a vase of lotuses home, but I left mine in the cab.

Grey and his friend Sex were going to some kind of class on Wednesday night, believe it or not, so I had to wade through the Welcome Back party at the Golden Calf for Tone Lather by myself. The joke was that Tone hadn't been anywhere, he'd been right at the bar for weeks, so it was a conceptual idea with a huge cake that said WELCOME BACK and of course some people didn't get it. I don't hate people like that, I just pity them. Everyone was issued an Instamatic camera with his or her crabmeat mousse so we sat at little tables and took pictures of each other pretending to be odd while we waited for the Pateena Glom dancers to stop whatever it was they thought they were doing on GC's suspended overhead transparent stage. Everyone calls the Golden Calf the Brazen Cow as a joke, but I think we should have a contest to come up with a funnier mean nickname for it. I am so sick of the place, even Devi said she'd rather stay home and she's a big party person (not referring to your weight, Devi, don't have a tirade and mimic me in your next video again!). We ended up at Sooey Generis so I assume the network of connecting tunnels has been completed. Now maybe the stoned guests won't get run over as much.

I know Thursday is Gay Night but just to torture myself I took Grey to Byzantium to watch them throw Chrisco Hackney up in the air on a beach blanket. They covered the floor with sand and the mood was friendly for those admitted. Duenna Veenil was livid when they said No Wrinkles Allowed but that just made her look worse, standing outside in the rain. Fortunately I don't have any wrinkles and everyone wants me to write them up. The excuse for the mousse was Chrisco's new Theoretical Show, which he kept alluding to vaguely, but not even the people buying into it know if it exists or not. Can you insure something like that? Anyway, he looked witty in his mismatched Pluteau St. Grisby socks and polka-dot shoes, and even Grey couldn't resist kissing him all evening and part of Friday. By then I was thinking of leaving, when Royelle arrived with Phil Willis and Danny DeNivea, who of course were photographing each other for their next issue of *Each Other*. They said I could interview either or both of them for it, but it's all I can do to get this written, let alone taking on more. I felt sorry for Royelle, hanging out with people who can't love her (and shouldn't) but not sorry enough to tell her who she was (something she'd taken on Wednesday had given her amnesia and she'd been wandering the streets buying clothes till Danny found her in Baal's trying on bomber jackets). I was tempted to tell her, "You're the spoiled offspring of a rich overrated Dad and Grey Gordian doesn't even remember kissing you!" but why make trouble and anyway she can read it here if she hasn't recovered yet. Otherwise it was fun except for Grey disappearing at the end there, but I'm not passing judgment till he reappears. I have my dupes of his videos about himself in the meantime, but it's not the same. If you're reading this and I assume you are, Grey, come back, you can bring Sex with you if you want. I can't face the mousse without you. Maybe that's what you're actually sick of?

THIS WEEK'S NOSTALGIA QUESTION: Who is the best-looking person I've ever slept with? (Answer to last week's: No, but I had a yeast infection that worried me.)

QUOTE OF THE WEEK: Leetha La Mount, accepting her Eppie from the Epidermis Council: "You're only aware of *yourself* during orgasm!"

CLOSING THOUGHT: My psychiatrist says thinking is like shopping, because "the mind is the world's smallest boutique."

P.S. Grey, please come back. I'll wear whatever you say.

World's Toughest Nostalgia Quiz

QUESTIONS

1. On *Kit and the Corporal*, who played the homesick Private Hooper, a bespectacled grunt who was always being sexually teased by Dora Zelling as the sergeant's wife? Hint: It's two people.

2. Tippo Squeako, "the saddest piece of wood in the world," was better loved than his human co-star, Barbara Moreland, when *Toddler Town* topped children's television programming in 1956. The little puppet went on to greater distinction, though, in the government of which nation?

3. Dull, super-patriotic Tax Boyd should have been a natural for endorsements, but what famous habit of his made it impossible for him to do television commercials?

4. Everybody knows Kippy Homonga was the immortal Choppers, but what blond-haired comedienne has also been known as "The Bite"?

5. What did Briny "the man who knows more than you could even guess" Harmon always do at the end of his *Education for You* program?

6. Porn queen Delicta Barnes can only be seen at home these days on X-rated videocassettes, but all through the Sixties she was "Your hostess with the toastin'est" for what brand of bread? Who does its commercials now?

7. No animal has ever won an Academy Award, but six have won Emmies—and not all for acting! Name them.

8. "There is only one Moundo Brown." True, but who was there three of?

9. It's hard to believe that Varla Kareen of current *Honeymoon Hassle* fame was once a tiny, unappealing unicellular organism. When was that, and on what series?

10. Who called television "a vast, empty parking lot"?

11. Someone successful once said, "My wife and I were married for the publicity, we're not in love." Who said it, under what circumstances?

12. Complete this classic Fifties jingle: "People may visit any time, so wax your floors—"

ANSWERS

1. Scrape Rathburn first played the part, but in the last season of the series he was replaced by his younger brother, Toby Rathburn. Incidentally, Toby replaced his brother three other times in major series roles over the past 20 years, including *Bachelor Mercenary, Hit That Howard,* and *The Youngish Attorneys.*

2. A trick question, maybe, because it wasn't really a nation. Tippo became the United Nations' official ambassador to children, an honorary post created for him and which he held proudly until his assassination in 1961.

3. He always insisted that the National Anthem be played in its entirety before his appearance.

4. None, to our knowledge.

5. He would point to a plastic model of a human head and say, "There's figurative gold in them thar hills. Good night."

6. Soapwhite Bread. Her contract was canceled when *Cockpit Candystriper* became a surprise commercial success. A funny robot with the voice of Marla Southman does the ads now.

7. Crullers, Mister Boggs, Miranda, Towzer, and Fitzi have been honored for their performances. Tattler won his award for writing the original story for *Three Strong Men*, a short-lived adventure series. Sorry, no credit for Houndexter, who was nominated for his role on *The Trashfords*, but lost to human Sterling Benedict of *Beats Me*.

8. Pvt. Benny Calbert, as portrayed by the Swensen Triplets on *I Split in Three* back in 1963.

9. It was millions and millions of years ago. The series was *Date Trouble*, but since television technology did not exist then, none of the episodes survive.

10. Jay Mantoff, before he went to ABC.

11. Oh, all of them, to themselves.

12. "—and keep everything spotless and always smile and don't ever yell or sit down or get undressed or touch someone unless, no, even if you're married to them." The ad was for Keeno, but they forgot to include its name in the jingle.

The Abandoned Lawyers

Once, long ago, though not so long ago that clothing styles were any different, there were two brothers who had the good fortune to be partners in a law firm, and if their hours were long, their hearts were still light, because they made healthy salaries. Their ancestral investments had left them well off, and between them they had more credit cards than there are things to buy.

William was the elder and taller of the two; he was the serious one, and always insisted that briefs be soberly bound in dark notebooks with metal clasps. No one knew the letter of the law like William, and although he seemed silvery and stern in the elevator, he was as fond of a martini in his sanctum as any giggling ruddy salesman. Bosco was the younger and more blithe brother; he loved expensive lunches and pretty vacation spots, and often forgot his anxious clients and hourly rate as he made garlands of paper clips to adorn his dappled secretary. The two brothers were unlike in many ways, yet were bound by the indissoluble girdle of blood and joint commerce.

One day their fame as lawyers finally reached the ear of the man who told the President what was happening. It was prompt William who answered the phone when the man called them, and he preserved his poise as the man explained that the President himself needed their help. Bosco, who was standing by, crowed happily and ordered a catered midafternoon meal to celebrate, but William knew that if the President needed help, their task would be a prodigious one, and so it was. In a poor section of the country,

it was hoped to build a nuclear power plant to offer jobs and inexpensive electricity to the people of the region, but the likeliest
site was owned by two willful children who were determined to
have their way in all things. Though only six and ten respectively,
the boy and girl were driven to realize what was after all the mer-
est crotchet of their delirious bedridden father, a widowed dotard
whose estate had devolved to his underage heirs owing to a freak
twist of jurisprudence in the local court. They planned, if the
mooning conjecture of minors can be called planning, to turn
their acres into a chinchilla farm, dashing the hopes of the hungry
and incidentally destining furry little animals for slaughter.

Bosco invited the children to visit his office, a typically ingen-
uous gesture that the youngsters twisted to their own ends. They
ate the provided ice cream and candies, but the elixir in the sweets
that was designed to render the pair compliant instead made them
crabby and tired, and they fell into a deep sleep from which they
awoke suspicious and resentful. They went away declaring that
the two lawyers were not to approach them again, and never even
acknowledged they had kept the gift packets of pencils and paper
Bosco had given them.

William chided Bosco for his inexact planning, but he could
never remain angry for long, especially with Bosco in his perfectly
tailored little suit. They resolved to go the scene to try to reverse
the court decision that empowered the children, but found that
many obstacles threatened their progress. The presiding judge in
the case had been bewitched by the girl's golden hair and the basket of flowers she carried everywhere with her. The boy, whose
lisp bordered on the grotesque, was deemed lovable by the old
black-robed pantaloon, who preferred to condescend to weakness
rather than be outraged and embarrassed by it. Worse, the children made a show of their propriety by calculated appearances at
the town's church services, and gave away pecks of green toma-
toes to their fatuous neighbors, who derided William and Bosco
and drove them from the steps of the office of records.

Left alone to scout out any misuse of their land that could

discredit the children, Bosco became downcast, and in his fretfulness wandered deep into their woods, a mishap he could have been spared if there had been a nuclear power plant on the property instead. When William noticed his brother missing, he realized the children would prosecute for trespassing if Bosco were discovered, and hastened to find him before they did. Luckless Bosco had fallen over some gnarled tree roots into a ditch, and lay helpless in the gathering dusk, keeping his tiny courage up by reciting possible suits he might bring against those responsible. When William found him, the moon had risen, and the slippery toads and serpents of the wood had begun to hector Bosco, to whose injunctions to cease and desist they seemed oblivious.

Just as William had helped Bosco from the pit, however, a rotten tree limb broke and, falling, knocked them both senseless. They awoke in adjacent hospital beds, having been prominently well-cared for and, through whatever persuasion, pronounced in excellent condition. The brother and sister had found them and taken them to the hospital, a stratagem that made any further hope to oppose the children appear churlish and cruel. How the brothers wept, knowing they had been tricked into an indebtedness that confounded their mission, and how bewildered they were, as legions of the shrewdly summoned media descended on them demanding brief recitations of gratitude and fealty. Bosco, unused to incoming duplicity, despaired, and told William privately he could pursue the case no more.

William, who was always intense, suddenly became more so, and collared his foundering brother. "Remember," he said, "that the world's population is increasing exponentially, and all these new souls will need inexpensive electric power to watch television. If we give up the search for more energy, chaos may reign!"

Bosco took heart and even offered to risk planting drugs in the children's well-guarded cottage. William did not take Bosco's safety lightly, however, and forbade it. Just then a telegram arrived from their office; William was summoned to the tropics on another prodigious case for the President. Before they parted, William gave Bosco a small electronic device engraved with the image of a lightning bolt, and said, "If you are ever in greater peril than ever mortal knew, turn this beeper on, and no matter where I am, I will hear you and come." With that he stepped into his helicopter and was gone.

Bosco had been instructed to hamstring the children's scheme until William's return by assiduously pitching haystacks of countersuits in the path of the delivery truck that sought to bring chicken wire and chinchilla feed buckets to the contested land. But, foolhardy, too adventurous for his lesser seniority, and giddy with eagerness to prove himself, Bosco decided to try to plant the drugs in the children's cottage while they slept in their beds.

The night was dark and cold, and the children's bodyguards looked heartless as they played poker on the bungalow's stoop. Bosco tried to lure them away with hired prostitutes, but the men insisted on being serviced at their posts. Then he made frightening ululating sounds, trusting that would provoke a rout, but the guards were jaded beyond any belief in ghosts, and quickly captured Bosco.

Since he had incriminating drugs on him, Bosco was charged with possession and jailed pending his firm's posting bail. The meal brought to him was so pallid and flat that he began to cry, but then he remembered his brother's signet beeper. Switching it on, he prayed his beep might be heard, and fell as if dead to the carpet.

Half a world away, William was exchanging gifts with murderous Berbers when he heard Bosco's call. Hurriedly excusing himself by pleading a concocted holiday, Respect for Energy Day, he shredded his agenda and jetted to the spot where Bosco was being brought to explain himself to the sneering press.

As it happened, the children were as crafty as they were beautiful, because they had fully expected William would come to relieve his inarticulate sibling, and they lay in wait to trap him with a disgruntled lawyer they had hired away from William's firm, a lawyer who had been passed over for partner in favor of Bosco, who admittedly was not that bright, delightful as he was. This lawyer, whose heart was a shriveled balloon of thwarted inflation, was prepared to reveal all the technical wrongdoing of the firm, to Bosco and William's broadcast disgrace. Sighting him on arriving, William paled and could say nothing, except repeatedly to request a martini. Bosco felt even more helpless, because William had always made the martinis and Bosco didn't know how.

Providentially, who should stagger onto the scene of the press conference just as the cameras began to roll, but the children's hitherto bedridden father. He had emerged from his delirium to find a renewed confidence in himself and his country, and exercised his option to resume control of the debated estate. His earlier distraction gave way to glassy sureness, and he ceded his land to the President. Checkmated by their own progenitor, the children stamped their feet and wailed chillingly, their own thorny ambition uprooted by its supposed gardener. Their display of downbeat emotion alienated the press, and the foiled pair were obliged to run away. As fate would have it, they were arrested at the Canadian border, when the girl attempted to transport her basket of flowers, and the potential parasites therein, across it. Given the way of the reformatory, the two probably came to a bad end.

As for William and Bosco, who had both learned a lesson, they returned to their offices, where they practiced happily for many years, though they came in less and less often as time went by. They both grayed impressively, and every year on their birthdays, a fine vellum card would arrive in honor of the occasion, apparently signed by the President himself.

Cast and Credits

DOOZIE MICHAELS (Maybelle) is the latest addition to *Endless Evening*. She succeeds Acacia Frond, whom you were hoping to see. Cyndie most recently made her mark as a Silent Maiden in *Ninety Silent Maidens* at the National Theatre of the Tall's spring clearance festival. She sang "Could I Be Wrong (About My Musical Ability)?" in the revival of *Hog Caller's Holiday* at the Short Pier Playhouse, and she played Lady Macbeth in Wilhelm Fistner's production of *Mother Courage,* despite Fistner's protests. She studied with Ova Eezie at the Hinterland Acting Academy and Grill, and toured with Pasticia Glamoor in *Everybody But Beppo.* Television viewers will recognize Doozie as one of the Krunch'n'Yum corn chips. Her films could have included *The Gall Garden* and *Hectic Are the Hungry,* but she was too young.

MICHAEL ROBERTS (The Old Mute) originated the role of Supernumerary in the Megalopolitan Opera's production of Sissi's *Redundo,* and has sung leading roles in *The Student Gypsy, The Nervous Widower, The Dull Bohemians,* and *Fat Starving Lovers,* even when no one was around to hear him. He trained with the Dodge City Light Opera, and was heard for years as Old Warden Feeney on the radio series *Those Careless Hubbards.* He has sung in several European countries that have crowned heads, and came very close to playing Will in the Parnassus-prizewinner *The Fire and the Flame,* but he is above all the petty politics required to get any actually good roles.

MICHAEL MICHAELS (Rocco) was haltingly introduced to Off-and-Partly-Under Broadway audiences in *Uh, Uh, Uh* at the Chelsea Driveway Repertory, following which he acted, directed, and sold intermission refreshments in *Vrroom, Chryslers and Native Americans, Women in Station Wagons,* and *Parking Problems.* His hair starred in the short-lived *Shearings,* which won the Outermost Critics' Circle prize as longest play of 1983. He could have made theatre history as Will in *The Fire and the Flame,* but the director wanted someone older to go with the badly miscast leading lady.

ROBERT ROBERTS (Lord Donnybrook) first delighted audiences with his now-classic Martian in the Men's Room routine in *Red White's Inanities of 1936* at the Old Paramecium Theatre. Besides his familiar ads for Otley elevators ("I'll be right up!"), he has charmed generations in light comedies like *Too Many Cocktails, That Tickles, Filet of Girl,* and *Let's Be Facile,* many of which he tours in annually, freely inserting speeches from one into any of the others. His film appearances have been many, though most of them were as R. J. Gatling in *Ready, Set, Dream,* the story of the Gatling gun. His son Bobby is currently television's *Teen Police Chief,* and wife Robbie runs the Robert Roberts Museum in Glaucoma, Washington. He would have been critically hailed as Will in *The Fire and the Flame,* but its producers wrongly assumed he would be touring in *Take That, Darling.*

GIRTHA MICHAELS-ROBERTS (Lady Donnybrook) burst on the Broadway stage in *More Pie,* but after surgery returned to the theatre as Lady Actwood in the Morpheus Theatre's reclamation of *The School for Secretaries.* No one who saw them will ever remember her classic betrayals of such roles as Madame Pouah in Bigtaud's *There Shall Be No Bottom,* Annelid in *The Polyfibers,* Violet DuVin in *Simmer in Sweat,* and most recently as Olea in *'Tis Pity She's an Actress* at the Allston Dead Play Arena. Her autobiography, *The Story of Her, I Mean, My Life,* with help from Jerry Hotchkiss, will be published by Pagan Books next fall. She asks that audiences bear in mind that stagelight adds twenty to forty pounds to the way you look.

VERNON LITTLEHOUSE (Playwright) has written numerous one-act, or less, plays for the Gravy and Hardtack Repertory Bus, including *To Be a Vernon, A Night with Vernon, Just Plain Vernon,* and *Let Me Tell You about My Operation.* He played the unappreciated artist in the premiere of his own play *Someone I Know* at the Corrugated Cardboard Alliance, and is accompanying tonight on the woodblock. He studied with the then late Norman Baker Woodworm at the My-T-Fine Correspondence Academy of Letters, and lectured on playwriting in his own home for the two years preceding his divorce. Do not ask him to brush a speck off his cheek; that is a permanent mark he is very self-conscious about. His new play, *It Hurts When I Climb Stairs,* won the first annual Littlehouse Award for Personal Excellence.

CLANTON CLANGER (Director) was the music director of the Stanford Dry-Ice Rink until its famous accident, following which he directed several modern plays in ancient dress at the Monadnock Art Round-Up, notably *Harvey* in togas and *Tobacco Road* in Restoration garb. For the Darien Volunteer Repertory, he has directed *The Would-Be Thespians, The Unfaithful Translation, An Ass Among the Donkeys,* and *The Country Climbers.* He has never stapled an actress to a stage flat, despite rumors to the contrary. Anyway, she survived.

HOODA THUNKETT (Costumes) is best known internationally for having hurled crabmeat mousse at Pluteau St. Grisby. She designed last season's Tijuana Shakespeare Festival, which included *It All Works Out in the End, If That's the Way You Feel About It, A Mountain from a Molehill,* and *Two Families in Different-Colored Tights.* Her tattoo designs for *Why Bother with Blouses* won the Epidermis Council's coveted Eppie. She was supposed to design all of Treena Pangoon's gowns for *The Fire and the Flame,* but her service evidently forgot to give her the message.

ZANE RODOMONT (Understudy) uses his abundant spare time to develop his hobbies—archery, ballistics, toxicology, and the occult. He has a shrill tiny girlfriend with an excellent loft for cast parties.

NOTE: Understudies never substitute for listed players, which annoys them. At matinees, the role of LADY DONNYBROOK will not be played very well; the role of A SWAN will be played by A DUCK. The operation of photographic equipment is illegal during the performance, but if you must, send the actors prints of any pictures that include them. There will be one ten-minute intermission, unless someone pulls the fire alarm again, which isn't funny, it really isn't.

Index

Aaaaaaie, as an expression of panic, 23

Adult games, antiquity of, 91

Affection, chances regarding, 2; how like rose, 61; as a sign of indebtedness, *see* Banking

Ahhhhhhh, as an expression of comfort, 24

Aiiieeee, *see* Aaaaaaie

Allegiance to the flag, 54; use in churches, 55

"Amazing Grace," as background music at political conventions, 55

Ambivalence, 56

Americanism, 55

Amiable veneer, 55

Amityville Horror, 18; as an American success story, 55

Amour, amour, 2–212; case illustrating, 3; being in love with, not with the real person at all, 34; as foreign-sounding hence menacing, 55

Amphetamines, as a response, 56; futility of, 57

Anger, as a response, 59; futility of, 60

Appearance, extremes in, 47; importance of, 55. *See also* Disappearance

Assiduous trumpeting of Americanism for own purposes, 55

Assyria, once great now dust, 164

Athletics, as arena for Americanism, 55

Atlanticism, decline of, 55

Atomic energy, 55

Attack, *see* Battle royal

Aztecs, once great now dust, 163

Babble, 72, 73, 74, 75, 76, 77, 78, 79, 93, 104

Babel, once great city now dust, 160

Mastodon, once furry now dust, 167
Maturity, misconceptions about, 82
Mechanisms, dangers of, 146; other than earthly, 146
Melting powers of alien lasers, 146
Mental giants summoned, offer selves, 146
Mercilessness, other than earthly, 146
Messy remains of mental giants, 146
Military summoned, 147
Mincemeat, other than earthly, 148
Modesty, *see* Heroes
Morale-building, 148
Mother, as a person, 110; as hostage of aliens, moral problems of, 149
Movies, people in, always knowing what to do, 3
Moving to a new city, 150
Myths, conforming to, 135–70

Naive new employees, 16
Names, remembering, 16
Nature, ubiquity of, 2–24. *See also* Insects
Neatness counting, 16
Night school, 16
Noble deeds, first sung, 16
"Nonetheless," first sung, 17
Nothingness, 17
Novas, *see* Sun

Oaks, apparent might of, 5
Obelisks, 193
Occupations, importance of, 56; list of, 57
Odds, *see* Fate
Office life, 57
Oil, 57
Opera, 57
Orphanage, 57
Oval Office, 57
Oxygen, properties of, 5–192
Ozymandias (Rameses II), 193

A NOTE ON THE TYPE

This book was set in a digitized version of the typeface called Primer, designed by Rudolph Ruzicka (1883–1978). Ruzicka was earlier responsible for the design of Fairfield and Fairfield Medium, faces whose virtues have for some time been accorded wide recognition.

The complete range of sizes of Primer was first made available in 1954, although the pilot size of 12-point was ready as early as 1951. The design of the face makes general reference to Century—long a serviceable type, totally lacking in manner or frills of any kind—but brilliantly corrects its characterless quality.

Composed by Graphic Composition, Inc.,
Athens, Georgia

Printed and bound by Fairfield Graphics,
Fairfield, Pennsylvania

Typography and binding design by
Tasha Hall